JUNGLE MAGIC

MOLLY'S MAGICAL ADVENTURES: BOOK TWO

V.K. MAY

Copyright © 2021 by V.K. May
All rights reserved.
No part of this book may be reproduced in any form or by any electronic or mechanical means, including information storage and retrieval systems, without written permission from the author, except for the use of brief quotations in a book review. To contact the author, visit: vkmay.com

Published by Opal Tree Press (2021)

Books in this series include:
The Magic Volcano: Book One
Jungle Magic: Book Two
Adaline's Magic: Book Three

A NOTE TO READERS

Molly Marsh uses American spelling.

She also uses the metric system which works like this -
    1 meter = 1.1 yards OR 3.3 feet
    1 kilometer = 1,094 yard OR 3,2801 feet
    1 centimeter = 0.4 inch

PROLOGUE

Book One, The Magic Volcano, started with Molly on a plane from Australia to Papua New Guinea. By reading articles on her tablet, she learned PNG is one of the most biodiverse countries on the planet with over 200,000 different species of plants and animals. Soon after landing, she befriended a blue butterfly as large as her face and when she arrived in her new home, her garden was full of the same bright blue butterflies.

Living in a hut at the bottom of her garden was a magical man named Yosia who brought a flutter of butterflies back to life after they had been killed by the wicked boy from next door. Using her own magic and charm, Molly managed to convince the boy there is a better of appreciating nature and making friends.

They fast became friends and put their brilliant science minds together to discover mysteries that even their parents knew nothing about. Starting with a contaminated lake that had leached through the jungle. Accompanied by a three-meter-long lizard named Ted, they discovered a second lake in the belly of a volcano. Intrigued, they climbed down and discovered plants and animals that should not exist.

Bit by bit they started to put the strange pieces together before tackling the most difficult question of all – what to do with this knowledge.

1

INTO THE JUNGLE

Molly treated herself to an extra swirl of maple syrup on her breakfast pancakes. It was going to be a big day, she knew. Yosia, Gideon and Eddie had gone to the volcano before dawn to collect samples from the lake, the gas cloud and as many plants as they could get their hands on. They all knew it would be dangerous work, especially if they encountered the flying monster known as the Ropen.

As Molly swallowed the first mouthful of syrup-soaked pancake, she replayed in her mind the part of the plan she and Michael had made. It started with her squeezing between the bars of the steel gate at the entrance to the mine, unlocking the gate from the inside, letting Michael in, collecting a water sample from the lake inside the cave, bringing it home, then giving it to Eddie when he returned with Yosia. Easy.

But it was almost midday by the time Michael was ready to go.

'Argh,' he groaned.

His face was as red as a tomato in mid-summer and sweat was running down his neck.

'Hey dude, what's wrong with you today?' Molly asked. 'We're only halfway down the street!'

Michael's hands dropped to his knees, and he gasped.

'Sorry,' he said. 'I didn't get much sleep last night.'

'Why not?'

'Mum was banging around most of the night,' he groaned. 'And every time the noise woke me, I started thinking about all the weird things we saw inside the volcano yesterday, and it took me ages to get back to sleep.'

'It was a very strange day, indeed,' said Molly.

She, too, had woken a few times, thinking about it. But now she was more worried about Michael. He was having a terrible time at home. His father was still in hospital and his mother had been under so much pressure at work, she had become unbearable. This made Molly feel more grateful than ever for her wonderful parents. She rested her hand on Michael's shoulder while he caught his breath. And she took a moment to look at the devastation caused by the earthquake two nights earlier.

The freshly painted houses and manicured gardens were no more than piles of rubble. She was glad no one had been hurt because she could laugh about the fact that only the posh houses had been destroyed. And the people who had lived in them were the owners of the mine. And it was the mining activity that had caused the earthquake.

Michael stood up, caught his breath, and looked around, too.

'It's kind of funny, isn't it?' he said. 'Considering the circumstances.'

'I was just thinking the same thing,' Molly sniggered.

As they continued down the street, Molly's eyes were on the thicket of trees she and Michael would have to squeeze through to reach the path that led to the entrance to the mine. Usually, the foliage was thick and scratchy and difficult to get through, but not today. With every step Molly took, she noticed several trees lying on their sides with their roots pointing at the sky.

'Watch your step,' said Michael. 'There's going to be a lot of—Argh!'

'What?' Molly said, turning around.

Michael was standing in dirt, up to his knees.

'I've just demonstrated my own point!' he said, laughing.

Molly was relieved Michael's sense of humor had returned. And even more relieved when they reached the wider part of the track. She stared at the riot of color and shape around her.

'It's so lovely here,' she said.

'It sure is,' Michael agreed.

'Did you know PNG has over 200,000 species of plants and animals?' Molly asked.

Michael nodded. Then his face fell.

'Oh no,' he whispered.

Molly followed the boy's gaze to one of the fallen trees. It was a frangipani. There was no mistaking the tree because of its unique flowers. Arranged like the petals on a pinwheel, they had a tiny pink dot at the center. Across the middle, the petals were yellow and at the outer edges, they were bright white. But now, the flowers were scattered on the ground and the tree was lying on its side.

'That was my favorite,' she cried.

But the ferns were still standing.

'It's curious they didn't fall, too,' she said, pointing.

'They're short and close to the ground,' said Michael.

Staring at the ferns reminded Molly of the day she had watched Ted scuttle between them before he had taken himself for a stroll through the jungle. He had been so confident and relaxed, as though he had owned the jungle. But since then, he had been changed by something unnatural in the lake at the bottom of the volcano and Molly was worried about the effect it would be having on him.

'You know, I—' she started.

'Shh,' said Michael. 'I just heard some voices.'

Molly listened for a moment, then shook her head.

'It was probably a bird,' she said. 'Lyrebirds are—'

'Shh,' Michael said again, clutching Molly's forearm.

She heard the voices this time. They were human. Adult humans. Probably their parents.

'You're right!' she whispered. 'Let's hide!'

With fewer trees still standing, they had to run several meters into the jungle to find a good hiding place. They lay on their bellies and peered at the path through the foliage. Molly saw an adult step into the clearing. Then another one arrived, followed by another.

'They're coming from the mine,' Michael whispered.

'So much for our plan to sneak in there and get the water sample!' Molly hissed.

A few more adults arrived.

'There must be nearly ten!' Molly whispered. 'What are they—? Oh, there's my dad.'

Molly could see her father holding his iPad in front of another man and two women. He was showing them something. A few more people huddled around him, and then a few more. Soon there were too many people standing around him for her to see him. But she could hear some of the words they were saying. Words like *mud slide, angle, extraction.*

'They must be talking about the earthquake,' Michael whispered.

'Oh, yuk, there's Jimbo,' Molly whispered, pointing at the man.

Jimbo was standing with his chest and belly puffed up, as though he was challenging anyone to step close to him. Even from her hiding place, Molly could see the sneer on the man's face. And she remembered the horrible moment he had pinned her against the wall in the hospital while telling her he would pull off her nose if she did not stop snooping.

Suddenly Jimbo started shouting at one of the women in the group.

'Typical,' Molly hissed.

'He's a nasty piece of work, that's for sure,' said Michael.

Molly had no idea what Jimbo was shouting about, but she noticed her father end the problem. He simply held up his hand in front of Jimbo and that was enough. Jimbo took a step back and shut up.

'Good one, Dad!' Molly whispered.

She sighed, then felt something hard under her rib. It hurt, so she had to move. She tried to be quiet but somehow managed to disturb a dry branch, and it made a loud *crack!* Some of the adults turned and looked in her direction.

'What was that?' Jimbo snarled, staring in Molly's direction.

Molly's heart pounded. She did not want her father to find her like this, so she held her breath and kept as still as she could. Michael did the same.

'It's probably just a tree kangaroo,' said one of the others.

The group returned their attention to the center of their huddle and continued to listen to Molly's father. Whatever he was talking about, it was obviously interesting to the other people. She felt proud of him, but ashamed of herself for hiding from him and spying on him.

'I don't think we're going to have much luck sneaking in there,' Michael whispered.

'Agreed,' said Molly.

'We'll have to come back another time,' Michael said.

But Molly did not want to give up on the mission so easily.

'Let's just wait,' she said. 'They might leave soon.'

Michael groaned, then rubbed his forehead.

'Yeah, okay,' he said.

2

PANGAEA

Molly felt as though she had been lying face down in the jungle for too long.

'This is ridiculous,' she whispered. 'I can't do this for much longer.'

'As long as they're still on the track, we don't have any choice,' Michael hissed. 'Unless you'd like to make an appearance.'

For a moment, Molly considered that option. It would have been easier. And it would have been nice to say 'hello' to her father. But she knew he would demand an explanation for her presence, and that would not be pleasant.

'I have another idea,' she whispered. 'Let's creep down the mountain, further into the jungle.'

Michael frowned at her. A palm frond was stuck to his cheek and a piece of bark was stuck to one of his eyebrows, which made Molly laugh.

'Why would we go further into the jungle?' he asked.

'Something to do,' Molly replied. 'And it would be a lot more comfortable than this!'

Michael sighed.

'Yeah, okay,' he whispered. 'Just crawl back slowly.'

Molly lifted her belly off the ground, rose to her hands and knees then slowly crawled down the gentle slope of the mountain. To her relief, she did not make any branches crack, and neither did Michael.

The further they got from the track the happier Molly felt. The foliage was thick, and its branches were long and wide, creating the perfect amount of shade. The air was warm and moist, and she could hear some bird songs. One made a sharp *cheep! cheep!* And another joined in with a *whoop! whoop! weee!*

'I love these songs,' Molly giggled.

She placed her hand on the smooth trunk of a tall, thin tree and looked up. The leaves seemed to burst out of the top of the trunk and arch up high into the sky before cascading down. And their thin tips pointed to the jungle floor as if to say: 'The ground is that way!'

'They look like giant umbrellas,' Molly said.

Michael looked up.

'Yeah, the big leaves catch the rain, then dribble it onto the plants below,' he said.

Molly returned her gaze to the jungle floor. The tree trunks were so dark, she wondered why the mushrooms growing from their bark were bright white.

'It's not very good camouflage,' she said, pointing at them.

'Ah, those things don't need camouflage,' Michael replied.

Molly kneeled on the ground and looked at the underside of the mushrooms. They were as white as snow, with thin pink stripes that started in their center and extended to their drooping edges.

'They look like umbrellas for fairies,' she giggled.

'Don't touch them!' Michael hissed. 'They could be poisonous!'

Molly stood up and brushed the dirt off her knees, noticing the tattered hem of her blue dress.

'I should have worn long pants,' she muttered.

'Me too,' said Michael, looking down at his red and bruised knees.

He took a few steps forward then stopped so suddenly, Molly bumped into his backpack. Without moving his feet, he slowly turned toward her, bringing his forefinger to his lips. With his other hand, he pointed to a high branch. Molly looked up and saw a magnificent bird with long orange and white tail feathers. Its chest was the same orange, and the top of its head was dark green with a little yellow cap on it.

'It's the Raggiana Bird of Paradise,' she whispered. 'A male one.'

Michael nodded.

The bird flew from the tree, its long wings and tail flowing behind, as though it was the star of a ballet. Then it landed on another tree amidst a group of plain brown birds.

'The females,' Molly whispered. 'They get to choose which male they want.'

The beautiful bird spread his wings wide, then dipped his head, bowing to the females. He fluffed up the feathers on his back, until they were shaped like a mohawk hair style, then sang *woo! woo! woo! woo!* The female birds watched him with interest but kept their distance.

'They obviously need a bit more convincing,' Molly whispered.

Another male bird arrived then gave a similar performance.

Soon, both male birds were bobbing up and down. One jumped forward, then backward, then forward again, while the other tilted his body to the right, to the left and back to the right again. A few moments later, each bird changed his moves to something even more hilarious, making it difficult for Molly to silence her giggles.

Eventually, one of the female birds hopped toward one of the males.

'He'll do,' said Michael.

The other females flew away, leaving the remaining male alone. He gazed down at the jungle floor and let out a mournful *eeeewp* that broke Molly's heart.

'He sounds so sad,' she said.

'Yeah, he does,' Michael agreed. 'But, hey, that's life when you're a bird.'

'I guess so,' said Molly. 'Let's move on.'

'Do you know where we're going?' Michael asked.

'Not really,' Molly replied. 'But as long as we can see the track, we'll be okay.'

She had a good feeling that everything was going to work out just fine, even though the jungle was getting thicker, and the air was getting warmer. She took her handkerchief from her pocket, mopped the sweat from her face and neck, then took a long sip from her water bottle.

'Isn't this nice?' she said.

'Yeah, it is,' Michael agreed.

Molly counted five distinct bird sounds: (1) *cheep! cheep!* (2) *ark! ark!* (3) *whoop! whoop! weee* (4) *choo! choo! choo! choo!* and (5) *eeoo eeoo eeoo.*

'How many species of birds are here, do you think?' she asked.

'There's about 800 species across the country,' Michael replied. 'But I don't know how many are right here, at this moment.'

'I wonder why we haven't seen any animals yet,' said Molly.

'They'll be here, hiding from us,' Michael replied. 'Rodents, possums, wallabies and—'

'Wallabies?' Molly echoed. 'But they're from Australia!'

'They're native to Australia *and* PNG,' said Michael.

'Really?' said Molly, feeling doubtful.

'Next time you look at a world map, you'll see where PNG was once joined to the top end of Queensland and the Northern Territory,' Michael explained. 'That's why the plants and animals are so similar.'

Molly thought about the idea of Australia and Papua New Guinea being joined. She found it difficult to imagine because she had flown across a vast ocean to get from

Sydney airport to Port Moresby airport. But then she remembered something she had learned in geography class the previous year - once upon a time, all the countries of the world were joined.

'Pangaea!' she said. 'I just remembered that word!'

'Yep,' said Michael. 'That's the name for Earth's super continent millions of years ago.'

'That's right!' said Molly. 'Western Australia was attached to India and the great Australian bight was snuggled around Antarctica.'

Michael grunted his agreement.

Molly tried to imagine what it would have been like to have been alive during the time of Pangaea. Being able to walk from one country to another would have been fun, she thought, until she remembered Pangaea had existed millions of years before humans had even evolved. Back then, there would have been nothing alive but dinosaurs and insects.

'I still can't believe we saw dinosaurs inside the volcano yesterday,' she said.

'Me neither, ' Michael replied. 'I was just thinking the same thing.'

'There's something very strange going on in this place,' said Molly. 'I hope Yosia, Gideon and Eddie are okay down there, collecting the samples.'

'Me, too,' said Michael. 'I hope the Ropen doesn't emerge from the lake and attack them.'

Molly had been worrying about that, too.

'I keep replaying in my mind the moment when the Ropen smashed its beak into the rock wall then fell into the lake,' she said. 'And I keep hoping it's still down there. Preferably dead.'

'Me too,' said Michael. 'But Ted survived lake, so it's possible the Ropen will, too.'

'That's a horrible thought,' Molly said. 'But even more horrible is the possibility there might be other Ropens. For all we know, there could be an entire ecosystem of the things!'

Michael grunted.

'Anything is possible,' he said. 'After everything I've witnessed since you arrived, I'm learning to expect the unexpected.'

'Hey!' said Molly, stomping through a mound of bark. 'You say that as though it's *my* fault all these strange things have happened!'

Michael was silent for a moment.

'I'm not blaming you,' he said. 'But you do have a way of making things happen.'

Molly was not sure what to think about Michael's comment. Was it a compliment or an insult, she wondered? She was not sure. She only knew that when something strange or interesting was in front of her, she had to explore it. She could not imagine living any other way.

She heard a crunching sound on the ground.

'What's that?' she asked.

'Dunno,' Michael replied. 'Perhaps it's — Er! Gross!'

'What?'

'It's those giant burrowing cockroaches!' Michael shouted. 'They're everywhere!'

Molly was almost too afraid to look down, and when she did, she felt her heart might stop beating forever. Scuttling around her feet were scores of black cockroaches, each the size of her shoe. She was standing at the entrance of their nest, and they were all charging out to defend their home like an army of shiny armoured soldiers.

'I think I'm going to be sick,' she said.

'Better step lightly,' said Michael. 'And fast!'

Molly ran behind Michael, trying not to slip on the bodies. She was not sure which was worse - the crunching sound under her feet, or the sensation of the creepy things running over the top of her feet. She tried to shake them off and run at the same time, but soon realized it was impossible to do both. Then she felt one scuttled up her lower leg.

'No!' she screamed.

'Keep running!' Michael shouted, a few steps ahead of her.

Finally, they reached a dry dirt path under full sunlight and there were no cockroaches to be seen. Molly brushed one from her leg then stomped on it.

'That was gross!' she shrieked. 'Honestly, I think I'd prefer to be captured by a Ropen!'

'Don't say *that* too loud,' said Michael.

3

A MAD DADDY CASSOWARY

Molly and Michael sat on a fallen tree, sipping water.

'Here,' said Michael, handing her a power bar.

'Thanks,' she said, dropping it into her pocket.

Michael ripped the wrapper from his bar and chewed loudly.

'Aren't you hungry yet?' he asked, with his mouth full.

'No,' Molly replied. 'Breakfast wasn't that long ago.'

'Yeah, it was,' Michael argued. 'We've been here for ages.'

He checked his wristwatch.

'We left the house two-and-a-half hours ago!' he said.

Molly felt surprised it had been that long. Then she realized how tired and hot she felt. She was worried about Yosia and his friends, too. And she started to think about Ted, again. Maybe he had recovered and was basking in her garden.

'We can head back home if you like,' she said.

But Michael did not respond. He was staring at something behind Molly.

'What is it?' she asked, turning around.

She saw a clump of ferns. Their fronds were slowly unfurling, as though waking from a deep sleep. And they were moving from side to side as though swaying to music.

'What are they doing?' Molly whispered.

'Dunno, but I'm going to find out,' Michael replied.

He stepped over to the ferns and gently touched one with the tip of his finger. Instantly, all the fronds huddled together, then curled back down to the ground.

'Collective intelligence,' Molly giggled, stepping toward him.

'Come closer,' he said. 'You should see this.'

Molly peered behind the ferns at a small clearing. There she saw a nest, made from leaves and bark, and at its center were seven eggs. They were a deep blue grey color and appeared to have a texture like leather. Strangest of all, their ends were pointy, unlike the rounded end of a chicken egg.

'Oh, wow!' she whispered.

'Beautiful, aren't they?' said Michael.

As Molly stared at the eggs, she imagined each one cracking open. Some tiny birds would wobble out and fall onto the leaves. Then they'd get up and take their first uncertain steps while squawking for their parents.

'I'm guessing the parents might be rather large,' she said.

'Yeah,' said Michael. 'We should probably leave.'

But they just stood there, staring at the eggs.

Molly saw some trees moving.

'We should *definitely* leave,' she said, stepping back.

She tripped on something and fell. Michael pulled her to her feet, then took a few steps back. Fascinated, they continued to stare at the moving foliage.

'Something is pushing those trees around,' said Molly, feeling her gut clench.

'Listen,' Michael whispered.

Molly heard a low volume, low frequency, reverberate through the trees. It sounded like a cross between the roar of an elephant and that of a tiger, not that she expected to see either in the jungle of Papua New Guinea. Then a big black bird, about the size of an emu, burst through the foliage.

'Cassowary!' Michael screamed.

He ran, but Molly could not move. She could only stare at the bird. It had a pointy bone growing from the top of its head, like dinosaurs she had seen in science documentaries and like the strange beast Ted had caught in the volcano the previous day. The bird's eyes were two yellow balls, each as fierce as the sun. Its face was bright blue, as though someone was strangling it. Two long red giblets, that would have hung down the sides of its throat, were bouncing from side to side as the bird ran toward her.

'Run!' Michael screamed.

Before Molly knew it, she was running. Faster than she had ever run before. Michael's round body was ahead of her, darting between the trees so much faster than she thought him capable of. The awful bird was behind her, the dull frequency of its cry rattling every bone in her body and making her wish she could drop to the ground with her hands pressed over her ears.

But she kept running. She could hear her own breath, gasping. She could hear Michael's, too, and the occasional grunt he made when a branch flung back and slapped him. She felt a tug on her backpack, which made her think the bird wanted something from it. She wished she could give her bag to the beast instead of running in terror. But that was not an option.

Michael started wheezing, like someone having an asthma attack. Molly prayed he could keep going for a bit longer. For how much longer, she did not know. She felt the bird tugging on her backpack again, so she thrust her shoulders forward and ran even faster. Somehow, she overtook Michael, then tripped. Michael's foot got tangled up with hers and, together, they rolled off the track, down the side of the mountain.

The fall lasted long enough for Molly to wish she could bang into a tree, just to stop moving. She stretched her hands wide, hoping to grab hold of something, but her fingers just slid off the rocks and whizzed by the shrubs. She could not see Michael, but she could hear him ahead of her, rolling, grunting, and crying out in pain. When it would end, Molly could not imagine. She only knew it felt like forever.

4

A DISTANT WATERFALL

When Molly woke, she felt pain on the side of her face. She lifted her head from the rock upon which her cheek was resting. It was grey, with a stripe of blood down the center. She ran her fingertips across her cheek and felt a lump and a small cut. It hurt.

'Oh no,' she whispered.

She pulled her water bottle from her backpack and took a long drink. Next, she dribbled some water onto a hanky and wiped the blood from her face. Then she pressed the cold metal bottle against her cheek and looked around. She was in a valley, surrounded by mountains. The skin on her face, neck and hands was sunburnt. The heat was pounding through her head like a two-sided hammer, and the glare from the sun was making her squint.

Suddenly, she remembered rolling down the mountain with Michael.

'Michael!' she shouted.

The boy did not reply, but she could see him. Sprawled across the ground, with his face buried in a clump of grass, he was a sad sight. Molly ran to him and shook him, but he did not move.

'Michael!' she shouted.

He did not respond, so she shook him harder.

'Michael!' she shouted again. 'Please wake up!'

This time, the boy moved his shoulder, then lifted his face from the ground.

'Mph,' he grunted.

'Can you sit up?' Molly asked.

Michael sat up slowly.

'Drink,' said Molly, lifting her water bottle to his mouth.

Michael took a sip.

'Thanks,' he croaked.

'Do you remember what happened?' Molly asked.

Michael squeezed his eyes shut for a few seconds, then inhaled deeply.

'It was a mad daddy cassowary,' he replied.

'Yes,' Molly whispered, her eyes filling with tears.

She felt relieved Michael was okay. If he had been seriously injured, they would have been in deep trouble. She could not have carried him home. Nor could she have left him there alone. No matter which way she thought about it, things would have turned bad.

Michael groaned, then ran his fingers over his scalp.

'Are you sure you're okay?' Molly asked.

'I think so,' he replied. 'Where are we?'

Molly looked around again. The valley must have been about five kilometers wide, she figured. It was flat and treeless, but the grass was green. Much greener than it should have been, considering it was under direct sunlight. And she was surprised to notice several clusters of wildflowers a few meters away.

'There must be some water nearby,' she said. 'And shade.'

'Dunno how we'll find the track again,' said Michael, looking behind him.

Molly followed the boy's gaze to the top of the mountain.

'We must have fallen a few hundred meters,' she said.

'I reckon so, too,' said Michael.

Then he looked at his watch.

'It's just after five p.m.,' he said. 'We might get home before dark.'

Molly tightened the buckles on her shoes.

'I refuse to fall over again,' she said, punching the air with her fist.

'Yeah, we could do without that,' said Michael.

Molly knew it was important to be positive and cheerful during difficult times, but it was hard because she was terrified. She did not want to spend the night in the jungle. It would not be safe, and her parents would worry themselves sick. Nor did she want to climb back up the mountain. It was too far, too high, and too dangerous.

'The best thing we can do is call for help,' she said.

'Righto,' Michael scoffed. 'Go ahead. Call for help. See what happens.'

Molly knew the boy was being sarcastic, but she tried anyway.

She stood up, took a deep breath, then shouted as loud as she could.

'Heeeelp!'

But her throat was dry, and her body was aching, so the sound she made was feeble. Michael laughed at her, which upset her, but she decided to ignore him. She stared into the distance. On the far side of the valley, she saw something at the base of a mountain.

'What's that?' she asked, pointing at the spot.

'What?' said Michael, slowly standing up.

'Over there,' Molly said, still pointing. 'The dark patch at the base of that mountain.'

Michael rummaged through his backpack, then retrieved a pair of binoculars.

'I didn't know you had those,' said Molly.

She stared at the boy as he pressed the lenses against his eyes. His face and neck were sunburnt, and his lips were chapped.

'Oh, wow,' he said. 'I think it's a lake.'

'Let me see!' said Molly, pulling the binoculars from his hands. 'Hey! There's a lovely white waterfall flowing down that mountain!'

'I was just about to say that before you rudely snatched the lenses from me,' Michael said.

'Sorry,' said Molly, returning the binoculars.

She took another drink from her water bottle, then returned it to her backpack. The heat felt so awful, she worried it might cook her brains if she did not find shelter soon.

'Okay!' she said. 'Let's get over there!'

5

THE APPLE GREEN VALLEY

Across the entire valley, the grass was the color of green apples. Flowers sprung up from random places. White daisies, yellow daisies and purple violas were mostly what Molly saw. When she arrived at a patch of hot pink flowers about as high as her ankle, she took a moment to stare at them. The petals were open and flat, as though someone had put them on an ironing board and pressed them. And their leaves were so shiny, they almost looked like plastic.

'I'm pretty sure my mum grew things like that in our garden in Australia,' said Molly.

'Hm,' said Michael, removing his T-shirt.

'What are you doing?' Molly asked.

'This,' he replied, draping the shirt over his head.

Soon Michael's entire head and neck were covered by the T-shirt, with only his eyes peering through the neck hole. His bare chest and tummy looked like a puddle of melted ice cream, reminding her of the alien in the movie

E.T. The Extra Terrestrial. Molly almost laughed out loud at the thought, but she was so tired and hot, she could only grunt. She lifted her handkerchief from her pocket and wiped the sweat off her face.

'At least we're getting closer to the waterfall,' she muttered.

'I can't wait to dive into that lake,' said Michael.

'Me, too,' Molly groaned.

She imagined how nice it would feel to take off her shoes and socks, then dive straight in. She would swim around, allowing every millimeter of her face, scalp, and body to get completely drenched in the cool, clean water. Then she would lie on her back and float while staring up at the sky.

'Can you hear the water splashing into the lake?' Michael asked.

'No,' Molly replied.

'I can't hear it, either,' he said.

'Who cares what it sounds like?' Molly scoffed. 'I just want to be inside it!'

'My point is, the water might be going down a sinkhole,' said Michael.

Molly thought that was ridiculous. Until she saw a large, dark hole in the ground at the base of the mountain.

'Oh, no!' she cried, dropping her head into her hands.

'It's okay,' said Michael. 'At least we'll find some shade.'

Molly hoped he was right.

6

THE SINKHOLE

Molly felt excited by what she saw. Three waterfalls were tumbling down the rocky wall of the sinkhole, forming a pool of white water at the bottom. She desperately wanted to be down there, soaking her hot and tired feet, but she could not see how to get there.

'Wow,' said Michael, staring down.

Molly looked at the internal wall of the sinkhole. It was made from several large slabs of granite in all shapes and sizes. Some of the slabs lay flat against the wall of the sinkhole, but others protruded from the wall, forming little terraces. Each terrace had its own arrangement of trees, plants, and flowers. A frangipani tree grew out of a crack between two rocks, and at its base was a beautiful green orchid.

Molly thought it was the most beautiful place she had ever seen.

'This is incredible!' she squealed.

She imagined her entire class from school having a

picnic in the sinkhole. Each terrace, she imagined, would hold a small group of her friends. And each group would see the other groups because the sinkhole was almost a perfect cylinder shape. It would be a magical experience for everybody.

Molly heard a bird sing *oooip!*

'What sort of bird is that?' she asked.

'Dunno,' said Michael.

The sound of the waterfalls crashing over the rocks made Molly's skin prickle with delight.

'How big is this sinkhole, do you reckon?' she asked.

'About one hundred meters down,' said Michael.

'That's about the same depth as the volcano,' Molly said. 'Let's hope there are no dinosaurs down there!' she said.

Michael laughed.

'I don't think so,' he replied. 'I mean, we can see everything from up here.'

'True,' Molly agreed. 'And I see nothing but rocks, trees, and water!'

'It's not the vast lake we were hoping for, but it will be nice to stand in,' said Michael.

Molly felt the sun radiating her scalp.

'The sooner we get down there, the better,' she snapped.

'All right, cranky pants,' said Michael.

'Cranky pants?' Molly echoed.

'Yeah, your tone was cranky,' said Michael. 'Just chill out a bit.'

'How can I chill out in this heat!' Molly shouted. 'My head feels like it's going to crack open!'

Michael took his T-shirt off his head and draped it over Molly's. The first thing she noticed was the scent of the boy's sweat on the garment as it hung down the sides of her head. It was not pleasant, but she was grateful for some relief from the heat and glare from the sun.

'Thanks,' she said.

'No worries,' said Michael. 'Let's get down there.'

Molly stepped down to a large slab of granite shaped like a staircase. She descended the five steps then stood on the last one, which hung over the bottom of the sinkhole.

'Now, this is a view to die for,' she said, stretching her arms up over her head.

'Speaking of dying,' said Michael. 'You should step back from the edge a bit.'

But Molly felt sure of herself, so she stayed where she was. To her left, she could see two thin waterfalls crashing over several large, moss-covered rocks. If she was standing on those rocks, she would be able to climb down to the base of the sinkhole but getting to them would be difficult.

'I don't suppose you brought a rope,' she said.

'Nope,' said Michael, sitting on the step behind her.

Oooip! a bird sang out again.

To her right, Molly saw a terrace made from a large, flat stone. The remains of a stone building, now overgrown by trees, was barely standing. On the far side of the terrace, Molly noticed a stone staircase that led to the bottom.

'That's the way we want to go!' she said, pointing. 'But how do we get there?'

Michael shrugged his shoulders, then dropped his head into his hands.

Molly knew he was just as sunburnt, thirsty, tired, and frightened as she was.

'Are you okay?' she asked.

Michael grunted.

A bird sang *oooip!* again.

'Oooip!' Molly shouted back.

Suddenly, the stone staircase creaked, then moved with a jolt.

'Hey!' Molly squealed, as it pivoted to the right.

Michael's face dropped, and his hands gripped the edge of the step.

'This is incredible!' he laughed.

Molly's heart pounded with excitement.

'Please take us there! Please take us there!' she whispered, clasping her hands.

A few moments later, the staircase stopped with a *thud!* less than half a meter from the next staircase.

'Yes!' Molly shrieked, punching the air with her fist.

It was an easy jump down.

'That was awesome!' said Michael, following her.

'It moved because I said the magic word!' Molly squealed.

'Do you mean that bird sound?' Michael asked. 'Try it again.'

With her feet safely on the second stone staircase, Molly looked up at the first one.

'*Oooip!*' she shouted.

Slowly, it moved back to where it had been.

'Well, isn't that interesting,' said Michael.

7

AN INCREDIBLE DISCOVERY

The wet mud at the bottom of the sinkhole seeped into Molly's shoes, instantly cooling her feet. She groaned with relief, threw her backpack against the wall, removed her shoes and socks, then waded into the pool. It was only as high as her knees, but it felt good.

'This is glorious!' she shrieked.

Michael leapt under the waterfall.

'Oh yeah,' he groaned. 'It's like having a shower, but a million times better.'

Molly sucked one of her fingers.

'This water tastes pretty darn good, too,' she said.

'Yep, it's definitely good enough for drinking,' said Michael.

He opened his mouth and allowed the waterfall to fill it. Then he threw back his head, gargled and spat the water at the wall.

'That's gross,' said Molly.

She filled her water bottle and handed it to Michael.

'Drink like a civilized person,' she said.

Michael reached for the bottle, but it slipped through his wet hands.

'Oops,' he said, lunging toward it.

The bottle rolled across the surface of the water. Against the current.

'Hey!' he shouted. 'Look at that!'

Molly watched her bottle continue to roll.

'What's going on?' she shouted.

'How is this happening?' Michael shouted, chasing the bottle.

'It's being pulled by something,' said Molly. 'But there's nothing there!'

The bottle kept rolling against the current, across the surface of the water. Suddenly, it simply vanished. Molly blinked a few times, then rubbed her eyes.

'What the heck just happened?' Michael shouted.

He took another step forward, but Molly grabbed his arm.

'Be careful! It might be quicksand,' she said. 'And I won't be able to pull you out!'

Michael scoffed.

'If it was quicksand, the bottle would have gone *down* instead of across,' he said.

'Okay, smarty pants,' said Molly. 'Off you go, then.'

She watched Michael leap forward with gusto. But he only got as far as the water bottle had then he seemed to bump into something so hard, it knocked him onto his butt, making a tremendous splash. Molly threw back her head and laughed out loud.

'What's wrong with you?' she said.

Michael looked up at her, his face wide with astonishment.

'I banged into something,' he said.

'It certainly looked that way,' Molly laughed. 'But there's nothing for you to bang into. It's just empty space.'

Michael scrambled to his feet.

'You do it, then,' he said.

'Okay,' said Molly.

She waded through the pool toward the place where the bottle had vanished. But she did not get much further than Michael had before she, too, was pushed back.

'You're right!' she said. 'It really does feel like I've just bumped into something.'

'I told you!' Michael shouted.

'I'm trying again,' said Molly.

This time, she closed her eyes, stretched her hands out in front of her, and moved slowly. A moment later, she felt something soft meet her fingertips.

'It's a wall,' she whispered. 'It's soft and springy.'

'It's not pushing you back,' said Michael.

'No, it's not,' Molly agreed. 'I think it's because I'm touching it gently.'

'Maybe you should step back now,' said Michael.

'But it's alive,' Molly whispered. 'I can feel it moving. It's breathing!'

'Get away from there,' said Michael.

For the next few seconds, Molly's hands felt as though they were massaging an animal. It was a sensation that reminded her of all the times she had stroked and massaged Kiki whenever she had wanted the cat to calm down. *Kindness and gentility, that's all it wants,* she told herself.

'This surface is *so* smooth,' she said. 'Oh, and there's a little indentation.'

Curious, she pressed her finger into it.

'It feels like gel,' she whispered.

She pressed her finger further into the dent, then the rest of her hand. A moment later, she felt her entire body gently pulled forward. Next, she was in another realm, a place she had never known before. It was soft and quiet. All she could see was something like thick liquid moving around her. She heard a *pop!* and a moment after that, she found herself standing in a place that was bright and light and filled with plants.

'It's a greenhouse,' she whispered.

The concrete floor felt warm under the soles of her bare feet. She knew she was dripping water on the floor, forming two little puddles that felt nice between her toes. She stared up at the high, dome-shaped ceiling. It was semi-transparent, made from an opaque white material that somehow let in the sunlight without revealing the sky.

'Amazing,' she whispered.

On the other side of the wall, she knew Michael would be waiting and wondering what had happened to her. She decided to return to him and convince to come back with her. But when she turned around to face the wall, she noticed it was covered in a thick turquoise vine that was blooming with bright white flowers.

'Hm. I don't recall stepping through that,' she muttered.

Molly gently pushed through the vine, feeling for the invisible wall behind it. A moment later, she felt it then heard the familiar *pop!* Next, she found herself standing in the pool beside the waterfall. Michael was there, exactly where she had left him.

His eyes were wide open, and his mouth was gaping.

'Wha—' he started.

'You have *got* to see inside this place,' said Molly.

'What?' Michael shouted.

'Seriously, Michael, it's *amazing* in there,' Molly said.

'In where? Where were you? Wh—' Michael stammered.

'Calm down,' said Molly.

'Calm down?' Michael shouted. 'You just disappeared! Then reappeared!'

'Just come with me, to the other side of this—' Molly started.

'This what?' said Michael. 'I don't know what's on the other side! There could be a family of hungry lions in there, for all I know!'

Molly frowned at the boy.

'If that was the case, I wouldn't have made it out alive, would I?' she said. 'Anyway, there are no lions in PNG. I'm sure you know that.'

Michael stepped back, lifting his hands into the air, and shaking his head.

'Suit yourself,' said Molly. 'But you're missing out on something incredible.'

She turned her back on Michael, then reached for the invisible wall again.

'Wait!' he shouted, stepping toward her.

'Yes?'

'Take me with you,' he said.

Molly laughed.

'Come here,' she said.

Michael waded toward her.

'Now stand behind me and put your hands on my shoulders,' said Molly.

Michael shuffled into place.

'Righto,' he said. 'What next?'

'Let me place my heels on the front of your feet,' she said.

'Ouch.'

'Sorry.'

'Okay. What next?' Michael asked.

'Just relax then slowly step us forward,' Molly replied.

She stretched her arms forward and opened her hands while Michael's huge feet moved forward. A moment later, Molly heard the familiar *pop!* then found herself back inside the dome.

'Wow!' Michael shrieked.

'Isn't it amazing?' said Molly.

'Look behind you,' Michael said, nodding.

Molly turned around and looked at the vine.

'Yeah, I know,' she said. 'It's the most amazing color.'

'I don't think the color is a coincidence,' said Michael. 'Do you?'

'What do you mean?' Molly asked.

She stared at the vine, slowly realizing it was the same shade of turquoise as the lake inside the cave, the lake in the belly of the volcano, and Ted's eyes after he had fallen in.

'You're right,' she said. 'There's got to be a link between these things.'

She noticed the vine's leaves were disc shaped.

'What the—'

And then she noticed the bright white flowers were growing from the center of the leaves.

'This is *so* weird,' she said, stepping closer to the vine.

'Yeah, it is,' said Michael, following her.

'I reckon they're bright enough to glow in the dark,' Molly laughed, reaching toward one.

'Don't touch them!' Michael shouted. 'We don't know anything about them!'

'Yes, we do,' Molly argued. 'They're hibiscus flowers.'

'No, they're not,' said Michael. 'The flower might be a similar shape to the hibiscus. But this thing is *not* a hibiscus tree. Also, its flowers are white, and hibiscus are pink.'

Before Molly knew what she was doing, she had plucked a leaf from the vine.

'Doh!' Michael shrieked. 'I told you not to touch them!'

Molly held the leaf in the palm of her hand, gazing at the bright white flower at its center. It had five generous floppy petals with undulating edges, just like a hibiscus flower. And the pistil protruded from the center, straight and strong, just like a hibiscus flower.

But there was something missing.

'It doesn't have any pollen sacks,' she said.

Michael peered at the flower.

'Whoever made it probably doesn't want its pollen mixing with other flowers,' he said.

Molly dropped the strange thing into her pocket, then looked at the grey concrete path under her feet. A moment later, she realized it meandered throughout the dome, separating each of the clusters of plants. Each cluster had its own unique look that seemed both familiar and unfamiliar. She saw a cluster of yellow and green plants. Beyond that, on the far side of the path, she saw another cluster with bright green pointy leaves that seemed to be opening and closing in a regular rhythm.

'Everything in this place is an experiment, isn't it?' she said. 'Just like the volcano.'

'It certainly looks that way,' Michael replied.

Molly felt her heart pounding.

'Do you think we'll bump into dinosaurs in here too?' she asked.

Michael took a step back.

'Maybe we should leave,' he said. 'It's probably not very sa—'

Molly heard another loud *pop!* then Yosia appeared.

'Ah!' Michael shrieked, jumping backward.

Yosia held up his hand.

'Relax,' he said.

Molly stared at Yosia, almost unable to believe her eyes.

'Yosia!' she shrieked. 'What are you doing here?'

Yosia's eyes darkened.

'The more important question is - what are you two doing in here?' he replied. 'Neither of you has permission to be here as far as I'm aware.'

Molly stared into Yosia's serious face, feeling a hard lump in the back of her throat. Whatever he was about to say next, she knew it was not going to be friendly.

'Your parents are very upset you've been gone for so long,' he said, glaring at her. 'Your mother was crying when she asked me to find you.'

Molly imagined her mother crying, and that made her cry, too.

'Ah, geez,' said Michael.

'We're leaving now,' Yosia said.

'Okay,' Molly sniffed.

She stepped closer to Yosia, in need of comfort. For a moment, she felt she was going to wrap her arms around his waist and cry all over his belly, as she often did to her father. But the man was looking so stern, she decided to keep her distance.

'How did you know we were here?' Michael asked.

Yosia frowned, then shook his head.

'We can discuss that later, Michael,' he replied.

Then he glared at Molly.

'I suspect you led the way in,' he said. 'Please lead us back out, now.'

Molly led Michael and Yosia through the wall, back to the shallow pool. The first thing she noticed was the sound of the waterfalls crashing against the rocks. It was almost deafening, after the silence inside the dome.

'Sit,' said Yosia, pointing to a large stone protruding from the wall.

Michael sat down first, then Molly sat beside him. Yosia remained standing, his face still stern. For a moment, Molly thought he was going to start pacing around like an angry lion in captivity. Instead, he just glared at her. Which was worse. Then he glared at Michael.

'What am I going to do with you two?' he shouted. 'You can't keep running off and putting yourselves in danger like this!'

Molly liked to think that Yosia was shouting to be heard over the sound of the waterfalls, but she knew it was probably because he was angry. She was too uncomfortable to meet his gaze, so she looked around the sinkhole instead. The pool of white water, the rock walls, the moss, orchids, and other plants that sprung from every crack and crevice were all so lovely, she wanted to stay there for as long as possible.

'Hey!' Yosia said, snapping his fingers in front of Molly's face.

'Sorry, Yosia,' she said. 'I am listening. I promise.'

'How did you know about this place?' Yosia asked. 'And why did you come here?'

Molly sighed.

'We didn't know about this place,' she replied. 'We planned to enter the cave in the mine to collect a water sample for Eddie, then—'

'I didn't ask you to do that,' Yosia interrupted.

'We know, but we wanted to help,' Michael said. 'Also,

we need a sample from the mine, if we want to prove that the contaminated lake in the volcano is related to the mine.'

Yosia sighed then put his hands on his hips.

'Continue,' he said.

'We couldn't get into the mine because the adults were in the way,' Molly explained. 'All we could do was crawl into the jungle, to avoid being seen by them.'

Yosia shook his head.

'This sneaking around and keeping things from your parents has got to stop,' he said.

Molly looked down at the muddy ground. She felt terrible about spying on her father.

'How did you find this place?' Yosia asked.

'We were walking through the jungle then we got chased by a cassowary,' Michael said.

Yosia gasped then pressed his hands over his eyes.

'You could have been killed!' he hissed.

'We know, but we managed to outrun the thing,' said Molly. 'Then I tripped on something and got tangled up with Michaels' foot, which made us both roll down the side of the mountain.'

Michael nodded.

'When we woke up, we were so burnt, we had to come here for shade and water,' he added.

Yosia ran his hands through his hair.

'This is very serious,' he said.

Molly looked into Yosia's round brown eyes. She saw anger and fear.

'You must never come here again,' he said.

Molly felt her eyes prickle with tears again. It had been a long day, and she felt exhausted. She felt bad about making trouble for Yosia, and for spying on her father earlier, and for making her mother cry.

'Do you understand me?' Yosia asked again.

'Yes,' said Molly and Michael.

'You two were in *grave* danger,' Yosia continued.

'We were,' Michael agreed, nodding. 'Please don't tell our parents.'

Yosia sat down, let out a long sigh, and stared at the waterfall.

'I can't keep hiding things from your parents,' he said. 'If you ever pull a stunt like this again, I will go to them and tell them everything. Do you understand?'

Molly nodded, feeling a fresh river of tears trickle down her face. She understood why Yosia felt angry, but she and Michael had not intended this outing.

'Yosia, could I please ask you a question?' Michael asked.

'What is it?' Yosia replied, his voice softening.

'How does this invisible dome work?' Michael asked. 'I mean—'

'That is not for you to know,' Yosia replied, shaking his head.

Michael pressed his lips together and dug one of his heels into the mud. Molly knew the boy felt frustrated. Like her, he always wanted an answer for everything. And the invisible dome required a lot of explaining.

'Does this place have anything to do with what we saw inside the volcano?' Michael asked.

Yosia sighed again then rubbed his face with both hands.

'I think so,' he replied.

'Did you collect the water and air samples from the volcano?' Molly asked.

'Yes, and I have a lot to tell you,' Yosia replied. 'But first, I need to get you home. Please return your shoes and socks to your feet.'

'But you're not wearing anything on *your* feet,' said Molly.

Michael glared at Molly.

'Not the time for making a fuss, Molly,' he muttered.

Molly pulled on her socks and shoes.

As they followed Yosia to the far side of the sinkhole, Molly felt relieved to have been rescued by him, but lucky to have found this mysterious place. She looked around again, promising herself she would learn more about it. Then she heard the last *oooip!* before stepping under another waterfall. Behind it was the dark rock wall and between two rocks was a large crack. She was not surprised to see Yosia step inside.

'Oh, goodie!' said Michael. 'Another cave!'

And he was right.

8

THE JOURNEY HOME

Molly followed Yosia through a steep and narrow tunnel between the rocks. It was almost completely dark, except for the glow of the green bioluminescent fungi. They were so bright, she imagined them on the ceiling of her bedroom, like the stars and planets she had stuck to the ceiling in her room in Australia.

'I didn't know this stuff grew in caves!' she said.

'Yeah, of course,' said Michael.

'I only knew about the sea sparkles,' Molly said.

'Sea sparkles?' Michael echoed. 'Oh, you mean the bioluminescent bacteria in lakes.'

'That's it!' Molly replied.

'They're completely different organisms, silly,' said Michael.

'Okay, smarty pants,' Molly snapped.

Yosia stopped in the middle of the tunnel, turned, and glared at her.

'I've had an exhausting day,' he said. 'And, just when I

thought I could relax, I had to come out here to rescue you two. I'm certainly not going to listen to you squabble.'

'Sorry, Yosia,' said Molly.

'Don't be sorry,' he replied. 'Just be silent.'

During the next few moments, the only sound Molly heard was Michael huffing and puffing behind her, bumping into the walls of the cave, and stubbing his toes. She tried not to laugh, but she could not help herself.

'Shut up!' Michael hissed, which made her laugh even more.

Molly decided that talking to Yosia might help her get rid of the giggles.

'Yosia, are we walking up the inside of the mountain?' she asked.

'Yes,' he replied.

'If it's the mountain I'm thinking of, it's about two kilometers high,' said Molly.

'Not long, now,' Yosia replied.

With every step, Molly felt more exhausted. Her legs were aching from the many hours of walking and running. And her heels were tender where the backs of her shoes were pressing against them. Her chest and upper back were sore from carrying her backpack, and her face hurt where she had fallen against the rock. She knew Michael was finding this part of the journey even more difficult, but she could not think of anything to say to make him feel better. Nor could she think of interesting to say to Yosia, so she listened to the waterfall racing down the outside of the mountain.

It was powerful and exciting, like the sound of a train

rattling over the bridge when she had stood underneath it on her way to school in Australia. Or the sound of the plane's engines just before it had lifted off the tarmac at Sydney. But the sound Molly wanted to hear most was her mother's voice. Just thinking about it made her cry.

Her attention was soon caught by a glimmer of light. And when they turned a corner, they were met with a strong blast of sunlight. Molly stared at Yosia ahead, framed by the light. He looked like a two-dimensional silhouette and for a moment, she could not tell if he was walking backward or forward. A few moments later, they were outside, standing on a narrow path that wound around the outside of the mountain.

Molly clung to a shrub, to stop herself from falling forward. Rolling down another mountain would be a bad way to end the day, she knew. The view from where she stood was wonderful. The apple green valley, and its tiny dots of color, was lovely. She could also see the waterfalls crashing down into the sinkhole, forming the white and turbulent pool she had been standing in, not so long ago.

'That's an amazing view,' she whispered.

'Wow,' Michael gasped, emerging from the cave. 'What a view!'

Molly breathed in deep, enjoying the fresh air.

'At least we're on the shady of the mountain,' she said.

The sky looked like an endless blanket of deep blue.

'What time is it?' she asked.

Michael struggled to look at his wristwatch while clinging to a crooked tree that protruded from the side of the mountain.

'Almost seven p.m.,' he said.

Molly heard the triumphant cry from a bird high overhead. As it glided down toward them, Yosia held out his hand and a moment later, the bird landed. Molly knew it was Adali from her garden.

'Hello, Adali,' she said.

Adali chirped a little greeting then hopped onto Yosia's shoulder and pecked at the whiskers on his chin.

'Um,' said Michael, still gripping the tree as though terrified he might topple down the side of the mountain. 'I'm confused. That's the direction we came from,' he said, pointing at a mountain on the opposite side of the valley. 'Why are we walking the opposite way?'

'This is a shortcut,' Yosia replied, stroking Adali's chest.

Molly and Michael exchanged glances then shrugged.

'Come on,' said Yosia.

Molly followed the tall man down the track, aware of Michael's heavy steps behind her. Soon, she found herself gazing down at a cluster of houses nestled among the coconut and banana trees at the base of the mountain.

'Is our street down there?' she asked.

'Yes,' Yosia replied.

Molly turned toward Michael.

'Can you guess which ones are *our* houses?' she asked.

'No,' Michael replied, clinging to another shrub protruding from the mountainside.

Molly thought of her parents down there, worrying about her, and she had to fight back her tears. She would have a lot of apologizing to do, she knew.

'Yosia, who else knows about the invisible dome?' Michael called out.

'No one,' Yosia replied. 'And we're going to keep it that way.'

9

A HOT BATH

By the time they stepped onto their street, the sun had almost set.

'Nearly home,' Molly groaned, dragging her feet.

'Mm,' Michael grunted.

Soon, the front door of Michael's house flung open, and his mother rushed out.

'Michael!' she screeched, scooping the boy into her arms.

'I'm okay, Mum,' he said.

A moment later, Molly and Yosia reached Molly's home. Her father was standing under the house, leaning against a stilt. His arms were folded, and he was glaring at her. Her mother was standing beside him, trying not to cry, and that was enough to make Molly cry.

She and her mother ran to each other and hugged.

'I'm so glad you're okay,' her mother cried.

Molly clung to her mother and sobbed.

'I'm so sorry, Mum,' she said. 'I didn't mean to make

you worry.'

Then she looked at her father.

'I'm sorry, Dad,' she sobbed.

But her father's expression did not soften. Not for a second.

'We'll talk about this tomorrow,' he said.

Molly knew what that meant - a long lecture, followed by a detailed discussion about all the things that could have gone wrong. It would not be nice, but Molly knew she would have to bear it with love and respect.

'Mum, I really need a hot bath,' she wept.

'Come on, honey, let's get you inside,' her mother said.

Molly was relieved to feel her mother's arm around her waist because she could not walk much further. Her body was aching, and her feet were blistered.

'Mum, I don't think I can climb the st—'

Molly felt a pair of hands on her waist.

'Come on, muppet,' her father said, lifting her.

'Thanks, Dad,' she said, wrapping her arms around his neck.

The next few minutes were a blur for Molly, perhaps because she had fallen asleep in her father's arms. She woke when her mother started to remove her shoes. A few moments later, she was soaking in a big bubble bath and telling herself she was the luckiest girl in the world. Even though her feet were covered in blisters, and her body was aching, and she knew she would not be allowed out of the house for a very long time, she felt deeply satisfied by her adventure in the jungle.

Her mother sat on the floor, dangling her hands into

the bath.

'We need to wash your hair, honey,' she said.

She massaged a blob of shampoo into Molly's thick hair. Molly closed her eyes and enjoyed the feeling of her mother's fingers rubbing her scalp. It was firm but gentle and it made her feel so calm, she struggled to stay awake.

'Hold your breath, now!' her mother said.

Molly held her breath as her mother dunked her head under the water. Her fingers ruffled through Molly's hair, releasing the shampoo into the bath water, then she lifted Molly up.

'There you go,' she said. 'Lovely clean hair.'

'Thanks, Mum,' said Molly. 'I'm very lucky to have you.'

'Yes, you are,' her mother replied, winking. 'Now, let me wash those clothes.'

As she lifted Molly's dress off the floor, a bright white flower fell from the pocket. Molly recognized it as the flower she had picked from the turquoise vine inside the invisible dome. She did not want her mother to see it, because she might ask questions.

'You're the best Mum in the whole world,' she said.

'Oh, you're sweet,' her mother replied, closing the door behind her.

Molly was still staring at the flower, long after her mother had left the bathroom. She found it strange that the flower was just as fresh and bright as it had been when she had first picked it.

'What are you?' she whispered.

But the flower said nothing.

10

TALKING UNDER THE TINY MOON

It was a warm night, but Molly was rugged up in her pajamas, socks, slippers, and a robe. Her mother had convinced her of the importance of staying warm. 'It will help your body and soul to recover from the shock of the big day out,' she had said. Molly knew her mother was right because every part of her body hurt. The backs of her heels were covered in blisters, and every muscle in her body ached. Her skin was tender from the sunburn, her headache was still with her, and when she lifted the ice pack to the side of her face, she felt a shiver through her entire body.

'I'm a mess,' she whispered, staring at the night sky.

The moon, which was the shape of a thick toenail clipping, provided just enough light for her to see the faces of Michael and Yosia.

'I still can't believe it,' she whispered.

'I'm not sure if I'll *ever* be able to believe what I saw today,' said Michael. 'A dome-shaped greenhouse, somehow made invisible, sitting in the bottom of a sinkhole in a deep valley surrounded by mountains.'

'And yesterday we saw dinosaurs in the bottom of a volcano,' Molly added.

'It's the stuff of science fiction stories,' said Michael.

Molly looked at Yosia.

'Can you tell us *anything* about the invisible dome?' she asked.

Yosia rubbed his forehead then groaned.

'It's a research facility owned by a company called Symbiotica,' he replied.

'Does the government know it's there?' Michael asked.

'Oh, yes,' Yosia replied. 'Our government accepts land fees from corporations like Symbiotica.'

'But does the government know about the invisibility thing?' Michael asked.

Yosia sighed.

'I don't know,' he replied. 'But I'm certainly going to discuss it with Eddie tomorrow.'

'Speaking of Eddie,' said Molly. 'How did you guys go today? Did you collect the samples from the bottom of the volcano?'

Adali chirped, then jumped up and down.

'It's okay, my love,' said Yosia, stroking the bird.

Molly had always suspected Adali understood what everybody was saying, but know she knew for sure. The bird was obviously upset when she had mentioned the volcano.

'I'd love to know what happened in the volcano,' said Michael.

Adali jumped up and down again. This time, her feathers were ruffled, and she was squawking.

'It's okay my love,' Yosia said again.

Then he glanced at Molly and Michael.

'I'll be back in a moment,' he said.

Molly watched Yosia walk down the garden to his hut. With Adali still on his arm, he entered. A moment later, he returned without her.

'Adali understands everything we're saying, doesn't she?' Molly asked.

She noticed an expression of surprise on Yosia's face when he heard her question. She also noticed he avoided answering her.

'Gideon and Eddie and I made it to the volcano just before dawn,' he said.

'Did you bring a gun? Or a bow and arrow?' Michael asked. 'To ward off the Ropen, I mean.'

Yosia shook his head.

'There's no point,' he replied. 'It's too fast.'

'Did you see it?' Michael asked.

'I'm very pleased to report, we did not see the Ropen,' Yosia replied.

'So, did you climb down to the bottom of the volcano?' Michael asked.

'Yes, we did,' Yosia replied. 'It's not an easy climb. I don't know how you did it, Molly.'

Molly showed Yosia the palms of her hands which were still covered in blisters from gripping the handles on the wall of the volcano.

'Oh, dear. They look painful,' he said.

Molly nodded.

'What happened when you got down there?' Michael asked.

'Well, the good news is that we collected several water samples from the lake, and a few samples of air when the gas cloud shot past us,' Yosia replied.

'Geez, you must have been quick to catch those gas clouds,' said Michael.

Yosia nodded.

'I think there might have been a bit of luck involved,' he said.

Molly remembered how quickly the gas clouds had shot up from the lake at the bottom of the volcano. She also remembered reaching the outer edge of the lake then stepping down to a grassy hill. At their base, the blades of grass were the same fluorescent blue as the lake. And when she and Michael had followed the little stone path into the jungle, they had noticed every tree showed signs of being fed by the same lake.

'Didn't you check out the jungle inside the volcano?' she asked.

'No,' Yosia replied, shaking his head. 'We were uncomfortable enough from what we could see of the place, so we decided not to wander through it. Eddie, however, took several photographs using his telephoto lens.'

'Awesome!' said Molly, sitting up. 'Does that mean there will be some photos of it on the news? I hope so!'

Yosia held up his hand.

'Don't get too excited, Molly,' he said. 'Eddie will have

to be very careful how he releases those photos and how he talks about his analysis of the water and air samples.'

'Will Eddie be at home now, analysing the samples?' Michael asked.

'Yes,' Yosia replied. 'He has a testing kit there. We should know the results in a day or so.'

Michael glanced at Molly.

'We really need to get the sample from the lake inside the cave in the mine,' he said. 'Eddie will need to compare the two before he can say anything bad about the mine.'

Molly knew that was true, and she was disappointed she had not been able to collect the sample earlier that day. *Tomorrow,* she told herself. *If I can walk, that is.*

'Just a minute,' said Yosia. 'Firstly, it's not our aim to say anything bad about the mine. We simply want to know what's happening to our ecosystem. Secondly, I have not asked you to collect that sample from the mine.'

'I know, but—' Michael started.

'Please listen to me. Both of you,' Yosia said, looking from Molly to Michael and back again. 'You've already put yourselves in enough danger. I cannot permit you to do any more.'

'But how w—' Molly started.

'Eddie will collect a sample from the mine,' Yosia said. 'And that's my last word on the matter.'

Molly thought that was unfair because it had been her idea.

'I'm sorry if you don't like it, but my decision is final,' Yosia said. 'You both need some rest from your adventures over the last few days and you need to stay out of danger. Do you understand me?'

'Yes,' said Molly.

Michael remined silent. The only sound Molly could hear from where he sat was the tearing sound of the grass he was ripping out of the soil. It was a nervous habit, she knew, like when he picked his fingernails. And it was so annoying, she wanted to slap him.

'Michael?' said Yosia. 'I'm waiting for you to tell me you understand.'

'I understand,' Michael replied. 'But I'm not happy.'

'I know,' Yosia said, his voice softening. 'But when you're an adult, you'll understand the importance of protecting younger people. It's part of the cycle of life.'

Michael stopped picking at the grass. He took a swig from his water bottle then lay down and stared at the sky. Molly lay beside him. The stars were twinkling bright.

'Yosia, what did you think of everything you saw inside the volcano?' she asked.

'I was horrified by the abominations down there,' Yosia replied. 'So were Gideon and Eddie.'

Abominations was a word Molly had only heard once before. She was not exactly sure what it meant but she suspected it might be the same thing as *unnatural.* She knew the plants and animals inside the volcano were unnatural and probably dangerous. Even worse, she knew, was the contaminated water from the mine. If it was leaching into the crops, or the people's drinking water, there would soon be a lot of trouble for everybody.

11

A FLOWER AND A BIRD

When Molly woke, she felt better. Her strained muscles had recovered, her sunburnt skin was calming down, and her blisters were healing. She stretched her arms high above her head and pointed her toes toward the end of her bed. Then she rolled onto her side and stared at the white flower on her bedside table. Still fresh, and with full and firm petals, it had refused to wilt. Molly picked it up and gently tapped one of the petals. The flower glowed, as though greeting her.

'Hello,' she whispered.

The flower was unlike anything she had ever seen before. Still sitting in the center of the bright turquoise disc-shaped leaf, it looked as though it was floating. Molly noticed a tiny point at the end of the leaf, where it had been joined to the vine. Protruding from that point, she thought she saw some fine white fibers. Thinner than a strand of her own hair, they were difficult to see, so she thought she might be imagining them. But when she lay the leaf upon the dark blue section of her Wonder Woman bedsheet, she could see the thin white fibers clearly.

'Amazing,' she whispered. 'It wants to grow roots.'

Molly brought the flower to the row of hibiscus trees in her garden. Their pink flowers were wide open and facing the sun like people lying on the beach, hoping to get a tan. As she got closer to the ground, the little white fibers were vibrating so much she knew she had to get them into the fresh soil as soon as possible.

She placed the flower on the ground and started digging. The soil was soft, dark, and moist in this shady position, so her fingernails were soon blackened with dirt. And as she lowered the flower into the soil, the thin white fibers wriggled with joy.

'You'll need some water,' she heard someone say.

Molly looked up and saw Michael standing behind her.

'Hey!' she said. 'Where did you come from?'

'I've been watching you from the edge of the garden,' he replied. 'I had a feeling you'd be up to mischief. And I was right, wasn't I?'

He handed his water bottle to Molly.

'Thanks,' she said, pouring a trickle around the flower.

'It's really pretty,' said Michael. 'But I don't think it will grow.'

'No, it won't grow,' said someone else.

Molly and Michael looked up to see Yosia standing behind them.

'Really?' said Molly. 'Why do you say that?'

Yosia shook his head.

'There's not enough sunlight down there,' he replied. 'More importantly, that flower was created to grow exactly where you found it. Not here.'

Molly sighed.

'Well, it seems happy to me,' she said. 'Please, just leave it here, okay?'

'Okay,' said Yosia.

He shrugged his shoulders, then walked toward his hut.

'Come on,' said Michael. 'I think we need to speak with him.'

As they approached Yosia's hut, Molly could see he was holding a piece of wood in one hand and a small knife in the other.

'What are you doing?' she asked.

'Making something,' he replied.

'Making what?' Michael asked.

'You'll see,' said Yosia. 'Please sit down.'

They sat on the grass beside Yosia's gigantic pumpkin.

Molly felt a gentle breeze around her face, and she caught the scent of the jasmine flower from a nearby vine. She heard the familiar *click-clack* of the insects in her garden and felt the dappled sunlight on her legs. Then she noticed Adali, sitting on her favorite branch in her favorite tree, watching them.

'Hello, Adali,' she said.

Adali chirped a little greeting.

Michael looked up at the bird, then at the surrounding trees.

'That's a very big tree!' he said, pointing at the coconut palm behind Yosia's hut.

'Yes,' Yosia replied. 'It's one of many planted before you two were born.'

'Before you were born, too?' Michael asked.

'No,' Yosia laughed. 'I planted them.'

'So, how old are you?' Molly asked, looking at the grey hairs on the side of Yosia's head.

'Old enough,' he replied.

He held up a tiny wooden bird. The detail was amazing. It was a precise likeness of Adali. Every feather, every line on her claws, and the shape of her beak were perfectly defined.

'Did you just make that?' Michael asked.

'Yes,' Yosia replied, twirling the bird between his fingers.

'It's amazing!' said Molly.

'It looks exactly like Adali,' said Michael.

Yosia nodded.

'It *is* Adali,' he said.

'That's incredible!' said Michael.

'I'm glad you like it, because I made it for you,' Yosia said, handing the sculpture to Michael.

'Really?' said Michael, a wide smile on his face. 'For me?'

Yosia nodded.

'But why?' Michael asked.

'To keep you safe,' Yosia replied. 'If you ever need help, just hold her and call her name. She will find you.'

'Wow,' said Michael, holding up the carving. 'Thanks, Yosia!'

Molly saw a ray of sunlight catch the edge of the carving and, for a moment, it seemed to glow. She felt jealous that Michael had been given such a beautiful gift, but she soon reminded herself she already had enough magic in her life. Michael, however, did not have enough.

12

YOSIA TALKS ABOUT SCHOOL

Molly and Yosia were in the kitchen, washing the lunch dishes.

'When do you start school?' Yosia asked.

'Mum said it will be next month,' Molly replied. 'I'm not sure what to expect.'

'Why? Haven't you been to school before?' Yosia asked, winking at her.

'Of course I have,' Molly giggled. 'But only in Australia. What's it like here?'

Yosia shrugged.

'Much the same, I should imagine,' he replied. 'But I confess, it has been a long time since I went to school.'

'How long ago did you finish school?' Molly asked.

'I was there from the age of ten to eighteen,' Yosia replied.

Molly felt surprised he had not started school until the age of ten because that was the age was now and she was soon to start grade five.

'Why did you start so late?' she asked.

Yosia stacked the dry plates on the kitchen bench.

'In my village, none of the children started school until the age of ten,' he replied. 'We had to walk a long way to get there and a long way back. It was too far for a small child.'

Molly imagined Yosia walking through the jungle for so long, he would have to stop for food and water. The classroom might have had trees growing through the open windows, and there might have been butterflies and birds fluttering around.

'What was your favorite subject?' she asked.

'Mathematics,' he replied.

'Oh,' she said, disappointed that Yosia would like something as boring as maths.

'Mathematics is important,' he said. 'It's the ultimate explanation for everything in our universe. Nothing makes sense without it.'

Molly knew that was probably true, but she was still surprised. And a bit confused.

'So why don't you do a mathematics job?' she asked. 'Instead of this one, I mean.'

Yosia took a long time to dry the next plate. Then he walked to the far side of the kitchen and put it in the cupboard, leaving the other dry plates on the kitchen bench. He rubbed his forehead, then flicked the tea towel before returning to Molly's side.

'It's a complicated situation,' he replied. 'But I—'

There was a knock at the back door.

From the kitchen, Molly could see Michael standing there.

'Hey dude,' she said. 'Come in.'

Michael shuffled into the house.

'G'day,' he said, nodding to Molly and Yosia.

This was the first time Molly had seen Michael indoors, under the fluorescent kitchen light, since they had returned from their adventure in the jungle. The boy's face and neck were bright red from the sunburn he had endured, and his red T-shirt was making him look worse.

'Your face looks like a giant, prize-winning tomato!' she said.

'Yeah?' said Michael. 'Have you looked in the mirror today?'

Molly realized she had not looked in the mirror for several days.

She ran to the bathroom, slid her plastic step under the mirror, stepped up and looked. Her face was still burnt, but not as red as Michael's, thanks to the many layers of calamine lotion her mother had gently dabbed onto her skin. But her right cheek was still swollen from her crash landing on a rock. It had a slight cut at the center, and a dark bruise was forming around her eye.

She decided she looked much worse than she felt.

As she walked back down the hallway, Molly knew she wanted to talk about something other than her face. Or Michael's face. She wanted to talk to Michael about school, because they would be starting together and traveling together, even though he would be two grades above her. But when she returned, she found Michael sitting at her dining table with Yosia, already deep in conversation.

'What are you two talking about?' she asked, pulling up a chair.

'I was telling Michael about the route to your school,' Yosia replied.

'Won't there be a bus to pick us up?' Molly asked.

Yosia laughed.

'I take it that's a *no*,' said Molly. 'Yosia, I want to know more about *your* school days.'

Then she looked at Michael and screwed up her nose.

'Maths was his favorite subject,' she said. 'That's all I know.'

Michael sat back in his chair and gave two thumbs up.

'Right on,' he said. 'Maths rocks.'

Molly was still curious about why Yosia worked as a house helper.

'Why don't you work as a mathematician?' she asked.

Yosia looked down at the table.

'I was offered a scholarship to study maths at the Australian National University,' he said.

'Oh!' said Molly, excited. 'Did you go?'

Yosia's eyes watered, and he shook his head.

'What happened?' Michael asked.

'I fell in love,' Yosia replied, a gentle smile lifting his face. 'And I got married.'

Molly felt confused. Her parents had never told her that Yosia was married, and she had never seen anyone else near Yosia's hut.

'So, where's your wife?' she asked.

Yosia smiled again.

'She's everywhere,' he replied, waving his arm around. 'She's a nature spirit.'

Molly felt even more confused, now. How could Yosia be married to a nature spirit? As far as she knew, that was a type of fairy. And fairies are far too small to marry.

13

IT'S NOT FAIR!

Molly inserted her knife into the gravy-soaked potato in the center of her dinner plate.

'Oh, yum,' she said, her cheeks bulging with the mushy vegetable.

Her father frowned at her.

'Don't speak with your mouth full, muppet,' he said. 'I've told you that a million times.'

Molly chewed the potato a bit more, then swallowed quickly because she wanted to speak.

'Did you know that Yosia is married to a fairy?' she said.

Her parents looked at each other, frowned, then laughed.

'Honey, what are you talking about?' her mother asked.

'Yosia told me!' Molly insisted. 'He said he's married to a nature spirit.'

Her mother nodded and smiled.

'I think that might be Yosia's way of saying he loves nature,' she said.

'No, he loves maths,' Molly insisted. 'But he didn't study it at the Australian National University because he fell in love with a fairy and married her.'

Molly's parents frowned again, but Molly continued.

'And did you know that Michael's dad doesn't want a house helper because he thinks it's wrong to have one?' she asked.

Her parents nodded.

'Mr. Calthorpe has shared his views with me,' her father replied.

'So why is Yosia our house helper?' Molly asked.

Her father put down his knife and fork and clasped his hands in front of his chin.

'It's a complicated situation, muppet,' he started.

'That's what Yosia said, too!' said Molly. 'What does that mean?'

'It means there's no simple solution,' her mother explained.

Molly did not understand.

'But if Yosia is so good at maths, he should be working as a mathematician, not a house helper,' she said. 'And he should have a nice house and a nice lady to be married to.'

Molly's mother sighed, then nodded.

'Honey, I understand what you're saying, and I agree with you,' she replied. 'But one day you'll learn there are some things in the world that are not fair. Not everyone gets the same opportunities.'

'You're one of the lucky ones, muppet,' her father said, ruffling her hair.

'Don't ruffle my hair, Dad,' said Molly. 'I've told you that a million times.'

Her father laughed.

'Okay, muppet. I'm sorry,' he said.

'So why doesn't everyone in the world have the same opportunities?' Molly asked.

Her father sighed.

'You're not going to let this go, are you, muppet?' he said.

'No.'

Molly's mother put down her knife and fork and gazed at her.

'Do you remember what culture means?' she asked.

Molly nodded.

'Culture is what a group of people believe,' she replied.

'That's right,' her mother said. 'Different cultures believe different things are important. Often this has something to do with the amount of money the country has.'

Molly was not sure what money had to do with anything, except for the rich people who had lived in the posh houses at the end of the street before the earthquake had destroyed them.

'Poor countries, like PNG, can't offer their people the same opportunities that rich countries like Australia can offer,' her mother explained.

Molly thought that was the most strange and horrible

thing her mother had ever said. She threw her knife and fork onto her plate, making a loud clattering sound.

'That's not fair!' she shouted.

Her father held up his hand.

'Don't shout, Molly,' he said. 'I've told you th—'

'A million times before!' Molly shouted. 'I know!'

Her parents picked up their knives and forks and looked at their dinner plates. Molly knew they were ignoring her because she had shouted at them. She knew that shouting at people was wrong, but she felt confused and upset because her parents had not given her a proper answer to her question. And her question was simple - why couldn't Yosia do whatever he wanted to?

14

THE MAGIC TREE

Molly woke to a *tap! tap!* She sat up and looked at her clock. It was 11:45 p.m. She was just about to close her eyes again when she heard the tapping sound again. She saw Adali hopping up and down on the windowsill and chirping like a firecracker. Molly could not imagine what the bird wanted, just as she had never understood what her cat, Kiki, had wanted whenever she had used her furry paws to pat her face in the middle of the night.

Molly closed her eyes again, but Adali tapped even more loudly.

'What do you want?' she grumbled.

Adali jumped up and down, flapped her wings and chirped for much longer than usual, so Molly got up and stared out of her window.

She could not see what the bird was so excited about. The sky looked the same as it had the previous night. There were no strange noises outside. And there was no one in her garden waiting to speak with her. She could not see any reason for being awake, so she returned to her bed and wrapped her sheet around her shoulder.

The cotton felt soft against her cheek, and the scent of lavender wafted through her pillow as she wriggled into a comfortable sleep position. She was just about to fall asleep when she realized she might have seen something strange in her garden.

She got up a second time and looked out of the window.

This time she understood - there was a soft glow across the garden, but not from the moon. It was coming from something in the garden. Between the two pink hibiscus trees, exactly where she had planted the little white flower earlier that day, was something glowing. It was the shape and size of a fully grown tree.

Molly rubbed her eyes.

'No way!' she whispered. 'It can't be.'

She glanced at the clock on her bedside table. It was 11:51 p.m., but she tip-toed outside. Then she ran straight over to Michael's house. His bedroom light was on, so she threw a small stone at his window, making a soft *ting!* sound.

Michael's window opened immediately, then his big face appeared.

'What?' he hissed.

'Get down here!' Molly whispered.

Michael nodded, then closed his window.

A moment later, he was running down his back steps.

'I couldn't sleep!' he whispered.

'There's a good reason for that,' said Molly. 'Let me show you.'

As they entered Molly's garden, Michael stopped and stared.

'This cannot be happening,' he said.

'You'll catch moths with that,' said Molly, closing the boy's mouth.

Then she grabbed his arm and led him closer to the glowing tree.

'You said it wouldn't grow!' she laughed. 'It must be over two meters high!'

Michael stared at the tree.

'It looks like a ghost,' he said.

'I know!' Molly whispered. 'I really want to touch it.'

'Me too,' Michael murmured, as though he was in a dream.

Together they stepped forward, their hands outreached.

'Stop!'

Yosia marched up the garden toward them, with Adali perched upon his shoulder.

'We don't know what's happening here,' he said. 'So please, don't touch anything!'

Molly knew that was probably sensible advice, just as Michael had given her sensible advice when he had told her not to pick the flower from the vine inside the dome. But she had done it anyway, and she was glad, because now she had a magical tree.

Adali chirped in Yosia's ear for a moment.

Yosia returned his gaze to Molly and Michael.

'Okay,' he said. 'You may touch gently. But only once.'

Molly leapt toward the tree with her hand outreached. But something pushed her back. Astonished, she looked at Michael.

'What—' she started.

Michael's mouth fell open again.

'That's what happened the first time we tried to enter the dome,' he said. 'There must be an invisible shield around this tree, just as there was around the dome.'

'You're right,' Molly whispered.

She glanced at Yosia, and saw that he, too, was surprised.

'How is this possible?' Michael asked.

Yosia shook his head.

'I don't know,' he replied.

He sat on the picnic blanket and stared at the tree.

Molly and Michael sat on either side of him.

'Have you ever seen anything like this before?' Michael asked.

Yosia shook his head, then leaned back.

'All I know is that the white flowers inside the dome glow at night, just as this tree is glowing,' he replied. 'But I don't understand how one of those flowers has grown into a tree. And I certainly don't understand how it's happened overnight.'

'Did you say you've been inside the dome at night?' Molly asked.

Yosia nodded.

'How? Why? Do you work in there?' Michael asked.

Yosia shook his head.

'I'm one of many people who are deeply concerned about the things happening inside that dome,' he replied. 'We've been watching and worrying, uncertain what to do, for almost a year.'

'You said *we*,' said Michael. 'Who else is monitoring the situation?'

Yosia shook his head again.

'I can't tell you that,' he replied.

Molly felt bad. She could see the worry lines crawling across Yosia's forehead. Adali, too, seemed worried because she hopped off Yosia's shoulder and wandered away.

'Let us help,' said Molly. 'Just tell us everything you know.'

Yosia frowned and shook his head.

'Starting with the dome itself,' Molly insisted. 'How was it built? Why was it built? What is the reason for the experiments inside? What will they accomplish? Why are they secret?'

She was about to ask one more question, but Michael pressed his fingertips into her knee.

'Ouch!' she said, swatting him away.

'Stop asking so many questions!' he hissed.

But Molly could not help herself.

'Yosia, is there *anything* you can tell us?' she asked.

Yosia shook his head again.

'I don't have permission to reveal any more,' he replied.

'But I do,' said an unfamiliar voice.

15

MOLLY MEETS ADALINE

Molly and Michael jumped when they heard the voice. It was right behind them. There was a woman kneeling on the ground behind Yosia. Her long, slender arms were wrapped around his shoulders, her beautiful brown cheekbones were glowing under the light of the magic tree and her large black almond-shaped eyes were as soft as a cow's.

'This is my lovely wife, Adaline,' said Yosia, turning to face the woman.

Adaline kissed Yosia on the lips. Then she stood up, straightened her brown dress, and stepped in front of the trio. Molly could see the woman was exquisite. She was tall and curvy. Her thick black curls sprung from the crown of her head, then cascaded down her shoulders like the fronds of a magnificent tree.

'Hello, Molly,' she said, smiling. 'And hello to you, Michael.'

'Wow!' said Michael. 'You're gorgeous!'

Adaline laughed.

'That's very kind of you,' she said.

She kneeled on the grass with her back to the glowing tree and gazed at the trio.

'How do you know our names?' Molly asked.

'We've already met,' Adaline replied, winking.

Molly glanced at Michael, then at Yosia, then back at Adaline.

'Yosia said he was married to a nature spirit,' said Molly. 'I guess that's you.'

Adaline laughed.

'I guess so,' she replied.

'Where do you live?' Michael asked.

'Among the trees,' Adaline replied.

Molly and Michael exchanged glances again.

Yosia pulled Adaline toward him.

'Please don't confuse them any further,' he said. 'They've been through a lot.'

Adaline sat with her back to Yosia then leaned against his chest. Her glorious black curls fell over his arm as she stared at the glowing tree.

'This was not meant to happen,' she said. 'But it's glorious, nevertheless.'

Molly and Michael moved forward, forming a semi-circle with Adaline and Yosia.

'What *was* meant to happen?' Molly asked.

'I really don't know,' Adaline replied. 'But I can tell you that the dome from where you stole the flower is a top security research facility.'

Molly felt her stomach flip when she heard the words 'stole' and 'top security'.

'Everything inside the dome is a secret experiment,' Adaline explained. 'You were never meant to know about it, and you were certainly never meant to see it.'

'Just like the volcano,' said Michael. 'And yet there were no signs at either place, telling us to keep out.'

'Good point!' said Molly. 'If these places are top security, why was it so easy for us to get in?'

'That's an interesting question,' Adaline replied. 'I suspect the shield around the dome decided to let you in, for its own reasons. As for the volcano - you were lucky. Or unlucky. Depending how you look at it.'

'That doesn't make much sense,' said Michael.

'The shield around the dome is an intelligent organism,' Yosia explained.

'Okay,' said Michael, sounding doubtful. 'But what about the experiments they're doing inside the dome? Are they doing research on seeds, or something?'

Molly's mind jumped to the Millennium Seed Bank. She had read about it. Built into the side of a snowy mountain, it has an underground storage place for the seeds from all the plants around the world.

'Is the dome a bit like the seed bank in Svalbard?' she asked.

Yosia and Adaline shook their heads.

'All the seed banks around the world contain the seeds of natural plants,' said Adaline. 'The dome you've seen is filled with things that are *not* natural.'

'And *this* is the most unnatural thing I've ever seen,' said Yosia, pointing to the glowing tree.

'Let's call it *the magic tree*!' said Molly.

Everyone stared at her as though she had said something idiotic.

For a moment, Molly wondered if she was dreaming. Perhaps the tree was not there. Perhaps Michael and Yosia were fast asleep. Perhaps Adali was sleeping with her head tucked under her wing. And perhaps she, herself, was curled up in her bed with her Wonder Woman sheet wrapped around her. But when she pinched herself and felt the pain on her sunburnt forearm, Molly knew she was awake, and the situation was real.

'Can you tell us more about the experiments?' she asked.

Neither of the adults responded.

'Can you tell us anything about that secret dome?' Michael asked.

Adaline sighed.

'Our government tolerates mysterious research and mining in exchange for the land fees it receives from those private corporations,' she replied. 'But, as guardians of our ecosystem, we dislike those experiments as much as we dislike the mining activity and all the problems that go with it.'

'Do you really think the mine is causing harm?' Michael asked.

'Dude, the earthquake!' Molly hissed. 'And the contaminated lake.'

Adaline and Yosia looked at Michael with sad smiles on their faces.

'We're aware that your parents work for the mine,' said Adaline. 'And we know they are good people. However, the mining activity is damaging the ecosystem.'

'But what does that have to do with the experiments inside the dome?' Molly asked.

Adaline and Yosia were silent again.

'Can you please tell us?' Michael asked, sounding as though he might cry.

'It's okay, Michael,' said Adaline, placing her hand on Michael's arm. 'No one is in trouble. But there is a lot going on, all at once, and we're trying to manage it in a way that's fair to everyone.'

Molly did not know what Adaline was talking about.

'But you haven't answered our questions,' she insisted. 'What are the experiments for?'

Adaline sighed.

'We only have some working theories,' she replied. 'Nothing definitive yet.'

'Can you share your theories with us?' Michael asked.

'Not yet,' Adaline replied.

Despite her fatigue, Molly felt frustrated. Adaline had not told her anything more than Yosia had. She glanced at Michael. His jaw was clenched, and he was grinding his teeth which, she knew, meant he was just as frustrated as she was. *We'll talk tomorrow,* she told herself. But for now, she lay down and rested her cheek on Adaline's leg. Then she heard the *click-clack* of the insects one last time, before she fell into a deep and empty sleep.

16

WELCOME BACK, ADALI

When Molly woke, the first thing she heard was Michael snoring. Yosia was sitting beside her, staring at the place where they had seen the magic tree during the darkness of night.

'I can barely see it now,' Molly whispered.

'Me neither,' said Yosia, stroking Adaline's back.

The feint glow of the early morning sunlight struck Adaline's black hair and face, making her look like a beautiful goddess from a Disney movie. She gazed at Molly and gave her a sad smile.

'I have to go now,' she whispered.

'Okay,' said Molly, rubbing her eyes. 'Where are you going?'

'Just watch,' said Yosia.

Adaline wrapped her arms around her knees and pulled them toward her chest. Her body curled into a ball so tight, Molly could not tell where her brown dress ended, and her brown skin began.

'What's happening?' Molly asked.

'Just watch,' Yosia said again.

Adaline's thick black curls flattened against her scalp.

'But, wha—' Molly started.

Adaline's hair straightened into a long, flat stripe around her body. Her lovely high cheekbones flattened, then her almond-shaped eyes shrunk down to tiny round ball shapes.

'Argh!' Molly squealed. 'Yosia, do something!'

'It's okay,' Yosia said again. 'Don't panic. This is a natural process.'

Molly could not believe Yosia had just said that. And she could not believe that Michael was still snoring. She reached toward him, intending to shake him awake, but Yosia stopped her.

'Leave him,' he said. 'He's not meant to see this.'

Adaline's chin receded. Her luscious brown lips flattened, then protruded, forming the shape of a beak. Then she threw her head back and let out a cry that rattled every bone in Molly's body.

'No!' Molly shrieked, clenching her fists.

Adaline's shoulders collapsed, then her legs shrunk, disappearing into her body.

Molly grabbed Yosia's arm and shook it.

'Do something!' she cried.

'It's okay, Molly, I promise,' Yosia said.

Adaline's skin thickened and prickled. Tiny black dots appeared all over her body and from each one, a brown feather sprung. Next, she shrunk to a brown feathered ball about the size of an apple.

Molly blinked a few times, then rubbed her eyes.

'What just—'

'Just wait,' said Yosia.

From the round ball a little wing opened and then another. Soon, Molly saw the body and head of a bird. The bird flapped her wings then hopped up and down.

'Adali!' Molly cried.

Adali chirped, then hopped onto Yosia's leg.

'So now you know our secret,' said Yosia.

'That's the most incredible thing I've ever seen!' said Molly. 'How did it happen?'

'Adaline is an ancient and magical creature,' Yosia replied, stroking the bird's back.

Molly remembered reading fairy tales about people turning into animals, and animals turning into people. They were always beings who had been alive for millennia.

'I guess that means Adaline is older than you,' she said.

Yosia laughed.

'Of course,' he said. 'I'm only a mortal man.'

Molly saw the wrinkles on the back of Yosia's hand as he continued to stroke Adali.

'How did you and Adali meet?' Molly asked.

'It would take a while for me to tell you our story,' Yosia replied.

'I'm listening,' said Molly.

'Do you really want to know?' Yosia asked.

'Yes!' Molly replied, clasping her hands together.

'Shall I tell her, Adali?' Yosia asked.

The bird chirped. Then Yosia smiled.

'Okay,' he said. 'I will tell you.'

Molly smoothed out the picnic blanket, then lay on her back. With her arms folded behind her head, she stared up at the pale turquoise sky. The sun was still rising, a new day was starting, and there was a warm breeze moving around her. It was the perfect time for a new story.

17

YOSIA'S LOVE STORY

'It was toward the end of my final year of school,' Yosia started. 'I had just turned eighteen and been offered a scholarship to study at the Australian National University.'

'How did that feel?' Molly asked.

'Exciting but frightening because it would have meant leaving behind everything I knew,' Yosia replied. 'My village, my family and the jungle, they were all I had known.'

Molly knew how that felt. She had said goodbye to her friends and her cat, Kiki, before moving to Papua New Guinea. But she had her parents, so she had not been alone. Yosia, she knew, would have been alone.

'Were you going to do it?' Molly asked.

'Oh yes, most definitely,' Yosia replied. 'It was an opportunity too good to refuse. It would have meant a top-class education, a chance to work on important research projects then return to my homeland with the ability to influence positive change.'

'What does *influence positive change* mean?' Molly asked.

Yosia sighed.

'Our country is very poor,' he said. 'This means we must rely on the wealth of other countries like Australia and America to create jobs for our people. And jobs are important, Molly, because they increase our standard of living - food, education, and housing, that kind of thing.'

'What kind of job would you have done?' Molly asked. 'When you returned, I mean.'

'I would have worked in a research or policy job,' Yosia replied. 'Or teaching, perhaps.'

Molly was not sure what 'research' or 'policy' meant, but she knew what teaching meant.

'You're *my* teacher,' she said. 'And you're great at it!'

Yosia smiled.

'Sorry, I interrupted,' said Molly. 'How did you meet Adaline?'

'I was walking home from school one day when I heard someone crying,' Yosia continued. 'The sound was so sad; it almost broke my heart. I knew it was a bird, but I couldn't identify which type and I couldn't tell where the sound was coming from, so I searched through the shrubs and leaves. Eventually, I found her.'

'Adali!' said Molly.

'Yes, it was Adali,' Yosia replied. 'She was in terrible pain. Her right wing was broken down the middle and bent backward.'

Molly cringed at the thought.

'I lifted her onto my lap while I figured out what to do with her,' Yosia continued. 'As I watched her flapping and falling over my legs, I started to understand what the problem was. The two main bones that form the front edge of her wing were dislocated, and they needed to be put back in the right place.'

'What did you do?' Molly asked.

'I gently took each bone between my fingers and wriggled them around until they popped into place again,' Yosia replied. 'Poor Adali screamed when I did it. But only for a moment. After that, she could open and close her wing with no pain.'

Molly breathed a sigh of relief.

'So what happened next?' she asked.

'Adali looked at me and made her happy chirping sound,' Yosia replied. 'You know the one.'

Molly nodded and smiled.

'Her wing was still tender, and she needed a few days of rest before she could fly again,' Yosia continued. 'So I carried her home and hid her in a dark corner of my hut, where the dogs wouldn't find her. I fed her a few worms and insects which made her feel better.'

'Gross,' said Molly.

'You may imagine my surprise when I awoke, shortly after midnight, to see the beautiful woman Adaline in my hut,' Yosia said, smiling.

'Oh!' said Molly. 'Even back then, she transformed?'

'Yes,' Yosia replied. 'She's been transforming since the dawn of time.'

Molly tried to imagine *the dawn of time*. It was an

expression she had heard in fairy tales. She had never really understood what it meant, but she imagined it was a very long time. Longer than anyone could remember.

'What happened then?' she asked.

'Adaline huddled in the corner, far away from me,' Yosia said. 'She was frightened and holding her arm because it was still sore. I told her I wouldn't hurt her, then I asked her to explain what was happening to her.'

Molly nodded.

'You may imagine it was quite a strange conversation we had, but I was so tired that I soon went back to sleep,' Yosia continued. 'When I woke in the morning, she had returned to the form of Adali the bird, so I thought I must have dreamed about the beautiful woman in my hut.'

Molly giggled.

'I carried Adali around with me everywhere for the next few days,' Yosia continued. 'At night, I would wake and speak with Adaline. With each passing day and night, I became more attached to her. It was a new feeling for me, and it was difficult because I was planning to move to Australia to study.'

'It must have been even more difficult because she is half woman and half bird!' said Molly. 'I can't imagine falling in love with a shapeshifter. I mean, what did you tell your friends and family?'

Yosia nodded.

'I must correct you,' he said. 'A shapeshifter is a being who can change their form at will. Adali does not have that control. Her form is controlled by time. From midnight to dawn she's in human form. Outside of those hours, she's in bird form.'

Molly tried to imagine what it would be like to have your body change so dramatically every twenty-four hours, whether you liked it or not. Even werewolves, she had read, only change their form once per month. On the full moon.

'Adaline is unique, isn't she?' she said.

Yosia nodded.

'In many ways,' he replied. 'After a few days and nights together, we decided we never wanted to be apart. Whether she was in bird form or womanly form, I needed to be with her. I felt as though she was a part of me, and she felt as though I was part of her. We knew it made little sense, but it was how we felt.'

'Wow,' Molly sighed. 'That's a true love story.'

Yosia nodded.

'So, did you really get married?' Molly asked.

'Oh, yes,' Yosia replied. 'We chose a time when she was in human form, of course.'

'Where did you do it?'

'In my village,' Yosia replied. 'My family, and the other members of my village, were there.'

'Did you wear something special?' Molly asked.

'Yes,' Yosia replied. 'I wore the traditional headdress of my village, made from feathers.'

'Ha-ha!' said Molly, laughing out loud. 'You wore feathers to marry a bird!'

Yosia laughed, too.

'But of course, no one knew I was marrying a bird,' he said.

'What type of bird feathers was your hat made from?' Molly asked.

'The long black feathers were from a cassowary,' Yosia replied. 'The short red feathers were from parrots and there was one long orange feather from a Raggiana Bird of Paradise.'

'Wow,' said Molly. 'I hope you didn't kill the birds for their feathers.'

'Of course not!' Yosia replied. 'We collect the feathers of birds that have died, and we store them for special occasions such as weddings.'

'What did Adaline wear?' Molly asked.

'She wore a headdress the same as mine, only smaller,' Yosia replied.

'What else?' Molly asked.

'She wore a top made from black beads and white shells,' said Yosia. 'And her skirt was made from cassowary feathers.'

Molly had no trouble imagining a bird woman wearing feathers, especially as a skirt.

'I'm curious about something,' she said. 'Does Adali's species of bird get along with parrots, cassowaries, and birds of paradise?'

Yosia shrugged.

'We have no way of knowing,' he replied. 'Adali is an unknown species. There's no other creature like her on Earth. She's completely unique.'

'Oh,' said Molly, feeling her heart sink. 'That must be lonely.'

'I think she does feel lonely sometimes,' Yosia replied.

He looked at Adali, still sitting on his leg.

'Do you still feel lonely, my love?' he asked.

Adali chirped. The sound was longer, and of a lower pitch than usual.

'Yes,' Yosia replied, stroking Adali's back. 'She feels lonely, sometimes.'

'Where is Adali from?' Molly asked. 'Maybe she could visit that place with you and—'

'We've been to Adali's birthplace several times,' Yosia replied. 'There are no other birds there. No fish, no animals, no people. Only the rocks and the lake.'

'I hope it's not like the contaminated lake in the cave and the volcano!' Molly said.

Yosia shook his head.

'No, the lake from which Adali was born is muddy and brown,' he replied. 'But it's surrounded by the most interesting cone-shaped rocks and a warm pink sky.'

'A pink sky!' Molly echoed. 'Do you mean like the stripes of pink we see in a sunset sky?'

'No,' said Yosia. 'The entire sky is pink. All the time.'

Molly tried to imagine that, but she was having trouble with the idea. Then she tried to imagine what it would feel like to be the only one of your kind on the planet. No parents, siblings, or friends. No one. Molly knew that if she was in that situation, she would feel lost and alone. And to feel lost and alone every day, since the dawn of time, would be unbearable.

But as she continued to think about it, she felt certain Adali must have some relatives somewhere. From everything Molly had learned in science classes, no one comes from nothing. Even the strangest and most unlikely creatures on the planet come from something. Even the Ropen, she thought, with a shudder, must have come from something.

'Can you take me to the place where Adali was born?' she asked.

Yosia looked at Adali.

'What do you think, my love?' he asked.

The bird chirped for a moment.

'She says she will give it some consideration,' Yosia replied. 'And when she is next in human form, she will discuss it with you.'

18

BANANA AND HONEY PANCAKES

Molly was stretched across her picnic blanket, feeling glad her head was in the shade because she had a lot to think about. Yosia's story about meeting Adali, and falling in love with her, was the strangest story she had ever heard. And the most beautiful.

'Hey!' she said, sitting up. 'Is that how you knew Michael and I were in the sinkhole?'

'What?' Yosia asked.

'Did Adali tell you we were in the sinkhole?' Molly asked.

'Yes,' Yosia replied. 'She flew home and told me.'

'Wow,' said Molly, lying down again.

The thought that someone, even a bird, could spy on her no matter where she was, gave her the chills. But then she reminded herself, Adali the spy had probably saved her life. And Michael's.

Molly could hardly believe that the boy was still sleeping and snoring.

'Shall I tell Michael about you and Adaline later?' she asked.

'No,' Yosia replied in a stern tone. 'People only encounter magic when they're ready.'

Molly looked at Adali again, then followed the bird's gaze to the mountains in the distance. Outlined by the golden light of early morning, they looked majestic.

Molly reached forward and stroked the bird.

'What are you thinking about, lovely thing?' she asked.

The bird chirped.

'Well, it's morning,' said Molly. 'I can barely see the magic tree.'

Yosia nodded.

'Not for long, though,' he said. 'In a few moments, the sun will be bright enough to make it completely invisible to our eyes.'

Michael made a snuffling sound, then moved his legs.

'Wake up, sleepyhead,' Molly laughed.

Michael blinked.

'What did I miss?' he asked, sitting up.

No one answered him.

'What are we going to say to people about this weird tree?' he asked.

'We won't have to say anything,' Yosia replied. 'It's barely visible.'

'True,' said Michael, staring in the direction of the magic tree.

The back door of Molly's house opened with a bang.

'Good morning!' her mother called from the top of the stairs.

She was carrying a jug of juice and four glasses.

Molly ran to the steps and helped her mother carry them to the picnic blanket.

Michael and Yosia stood up.

'Good morning, Mrs. Marsh,' said Michael.

'Hello, Michael,' she replied. 'Hello, Yosia.'

'Good morning, Mrs. Marsh,' Yosia replied.

'Sit next to me, Mum,' said Molly.

Before Molly's mother landed on the blanket, Molly had wrapped her arms around her.

'You smell of sugar and lemons,' she said.

Her mother laughed, then gazed around the garden.

'It's lovely here,' she said.

Molly wondered if her mother had seen the magic tree glowing during the night.

'We have such a beautiful range of trees and flowers here, don't we?' her mother said.

'Mm,' said Molly, Michael and Yosia.

'The butterflies and birds are lovely too,' her mother added.

Adali hopped onto the edge of Molly's mother's glass and took a sip of her juice.

'Oh, you're welcome, little birdie,' she said, laughing.

She looked straight ahead at the place where the magic tree had been visible.

'Those pink hibiscus flowers are magnificent in this light,' she said.

Molly, Michael, and Yosia glanced at each other again.

'What are you looking at, Mum?' Molly asked.

'Those two pink hibiscus trees,' she replied, pointing at them. 'Straight ahead, Molly.'

Molly gasped and laughed at the same time, which made her cough.

'Are you all right, honey?' her mother asked, patting her on the back.

'I'm fine, thanks, Mum,' said Molly.

Adali hopped onto Molly's mother's knee and chirped at her.

'You have my attention, little birdie,' she said, smiling.

Adali flew straight toward the magic tree then disappeared.

'Where did that little bird go?' Molly's mother asked.

No one replied.

Molly and Michael exchanged glances. Molly knew he was thinking the same thing she was thinking - just like the shield around the dome that had made her water bottle invisible, there was a shield around the magic tree, and it had just made Adali invisible.

Molly's mother stood up and stretched.

'I'm going inside to make pancakes,' she said. 'Who wants one?'

'Me!' said Molly and Michael.

As Molly watched her mother return to the house, she felt her eyes prickle with tears. She knew she would never be able to share this incredible magic with her mother because her mother simply would not understand what she was saying.

'Are you okay?' Yosia asked.

Molly sniffed, then nodded.

'My mum doesn't believe in magic,' she said.

'Don't feel bad about that,' said Yosia. 'Magic isn't for everyone.'

'Hang on a minute,' said Michael, straightening his T-shirt. 'I don't believe in magic, and I saw the glowing tree.'

'Yeah, but you're weird,' Molly replied.

'That's not very nice,' said Yosia.

'Sorry,' said Molly. 'You're not weird. You do believe in magic. You just don't know it yet.'

As they walked toward the back steps of the house, it occurred to Molly that growing up was probably going to involve learning more things that her parents would not understand. She was not happy about that because she loved them so much, she wanted to share everything with them. For now, though, her mother's banana and honey pancakes were all that mattered.

19

MOLLY LOVES ADALI

When Molly woke from her afternoon nap, she thought she was back home in Australia for just a moment. She expected her cat, Kiki, to tap her face with her little black paw, or to make that cute little *prring!* sound. But neither of those things happened because Kiki was in Australia and Molly was in Papua New Guinea.

Even though Molly had been there for a few nights, she was still missing Kiki. Especially at night, which was when the cat would lie on top of her and purr. More than anything, she wanted to be with Kiki, to wrap her arms around her and care for her. But for now, she could at least console herself with the knowledge that Kiki was safe with her Aunty Dindi.

Molly wandered into the kitchen.

'Mum, do we have any cold, fizzy drink?' she asked, holding open the door of the fridge.

She did not hear her mother's answer, so she wandered into the lounge room, but her mother was not there. Nor was she in the bathroom or her bedroom. Her father was not around, either.

When Molly opened the back door, she saw them lazing on her picnic blanket under the shade of the hibiscus trees that separated her garden from Michael's garden. Both had high pillows under their heads and were reading.

'Hey, muppet,' her father said, looking up from his tablet.

'Hey, Dad!' Molly called out. 'Do we have any fizzy drink?'

'Yes, it's on the —' her father started.

'I'll get it for her,' said Yosia, dropping his rake.

He was shiny with sweat, but somehow, Adali managed to grip his shoulder. Molly held the back door open for him, then she sat at the table, staring into space. Still struggling to wake up, she could not think of anything to say, not even 'thank you' when Yosia placed the bubbling drink in front of her. She had to take a few sips before she woke up enough to be polite.

'Ah!' she said. 'Thanks, Yosia. I love ginger beer.'

Yosia sat down, then wiped his face with the corner of his shirt. Adali hopped off his shoulder then wandered into the center of the table. As Molly stared at the lovely bird, she realized Adali was standing on the exact spot where her mother always placed the dinner. And in that moment, Molly knew she would never eat roast chicken, or turkey, or any bird ever again.

20

ADALI SHOWS MOLLY A TRICK

Staring at the night sky made Molly feel happy. Even though the swirls and sparkles of the outer edge of the Milky Way were not visible on this evening, she was enjoying the deep indigo color, the sprinkling of stars and the almost quarter moon. The magic tree was glowing faintly. So faintly, she knew her parents might not notice it, even if they did wander outside.

Yosia was lying beside Molly, so when she glanced at him, she saw his profile. It was a face she found interesting. His thick curly hair seemed to bounce up from his forehead as though telling the sky where he was. And his nose, which was thick and round, almost looked like a beak. Molly found that very amusing, considering he had married a bird.

Then she noticed Adali staring at the sky, too. The back of her little feathered head was resting in the palm of Yosia's hand. Her little belly was pointing upward, and she was staring at the sky, just like everybody else. It looked so funny; Molly burst out laughing.

Yosia laughed, too.

'My lovely Adali,' he whispered.

Molly sat up and looked at him.

'Yosia, could you please tell me how Adali flew through the shield around the magic tree this morning?' she asked. 'I mean, we all saw it. Except for Mum, of course. But Michael, you and I saw it. It was incredible!'

Yosia wriggled his fingers, making the bird's head bob up and down.

'What do you think, Adali?' he asked. 'Should we show Molly how it's done?'

Adali sat up and chirped, as if to say: 'Okay, watch this.'

She stood on the grass and moved her head from side to side, as though getting ready. Then she flapped her wings and started to fly toward the magic tree. Suddenly, Molly had a feeling of heaviness. She could see every beat of the bird's wings as though she was watching a documentary that deliberately showed everything in slow motion so the viewer could understand what they were looking at.

'What's happening?' Molly asked, hearing her voice in slow motion, like a vinyl record being played at a speed too slow.

She saw a soft glow around Adali, the same glow that surrounded the magic tree. And as Adali got closer to the tree, Molly started to see its shield. It was almost transparent, but not completely. It looked as though it was filled with a thick, clear gel and it was expanding and contracting, like a creature breathing in and out.

'It's alive,' Molly whispered. 'Just like the wall around the dome.'

She noticed the outer edge of the shield had several small holes that opened and closed with each breath. And Adali seemed to know exactly where and when the next hole would appear because she flew straight through.

'Incredible,' Molly whispered.

The bird wrapped her claws around a branch, then folded her wings and looked at Molly. Suddenly, everything returned to normal. Time returned to its usual pace and the shield was once again invisible. All Molly could see was a faint ghost of a tree and a faint ghost of a bird sitting upon one of its branches.

'I must be dreaming,' she said.

'You're awake,' said Yosia.

'That was magic,' said Molly. 'You can't tell me that was science. That was magic!'

'They are the same thing,' said Yosia.

Then he turned his attention to Adali.

'Come back, my love,' he called out.

Adali flew straight through the invisible shield, then landed on Yosia's knee and chirped.

'Thank you, Adali,' said Molly. 'That was amazing.'

Adali cheeped again.

Yosia looked at Molly.

'The purpose of this demonstration was to answer your question about how Adali flies through the shield,' he said. 'This is *not* for you to attempt.'

Molly laughed.

'As if I could do *that*!' she said.

But as Molly gazed at the magic tree, she wondered if it might be possible for her to do what Adali had just done. If Yosia was right - that magic is science we have not yet understood - then Molly might be able to figure out how to squeeze through a hole in the shield at exactly the right moment, just as Adali had done. She glanced at Adali, only to find the bird already watching her.

The bird winked at Molly, fluffed up her feathers then tucked her head under her wing.

21

MOLLY'S NIGHTMARE

Molly was dreaming she was walking through a tunnel deep under the ground. The walls, ceiling, and floor were made from a golden rock containing millions of turquoise and white stones. They sparkled so brightly she wondered if they were diamonds, but there was no one to ask. She felt the tunnel breathing. It was alive, like a giant blood vessel inside the body of a great God.

In front of Molly, a leaf emerged from the ground, then grew into a tree. Like the stones, its trunk was a golden color, its leaves were turquoise, and its flowers were white. A branch extended toward her. Upon it sat a brown, furry creature eating a mango. She asked the creature which way she should go next, but it was too busy eating to answer.

When it finally swallowed the last bite, it threw the stone onto the floor. There, another tree sprouted up and grew to full size. Molly asked again which way she should go. This time, the creature responded by pointing one of its sharp brown claws in one direction, and its thick golden tail in the opposite direction.

Molly decided to let her body take her where it wanted to go.

She arrived at a circular space. Two round people emerged from the rock. Wearing yellow hats and blue overalls that barely reached around their fat tummies, they looked like twins. They stepped from side to side, waving their arms and singing. Then they jumped toward each other, their fat bellies colliding and making them fall to the floor. But like rubber balls, they bounced back. Next, they juggled two shiny golden keys between them. Soon, it was four, then eight, then Molly lost count.

'Choose the right key, and you'll go free!' one of them sang.

'Choose the wrong one, and we'll have some fun!' sang the other.

A screeching sound rang through the tunnel as a small brown bird flew between the jugglers. It grabbed one of the golden keys in its beak, then dropped it at Molly's feet. She picked it up and followed the bird through an ever-changing network of tunnels. Like a sleeping beast, the network expanded and contracted. With each inhalation, a new tunnel appeared, then disappeared with each exhalation. Molly could have gone in any direction, but she followed the bird.

A clear glass door appeared, occupying the entire tunnel, and the bird flew straight through. Molly knew she could not do the same, so she stretched her arm forward and thrust the key into its lock. She heard a click, then the door moved forward, around her and through her. She was on the other side, staring at a dull grey room.

The scent of blood filled her head, and the sound of screaming hurt her ears. She saw a long queue of cows, pigs and sheep descending a ramp. It was an automatic ramp, like a conveyer belt at a check-out station in a supermarket. The animals could not make it stop. They could only stand there, moving closer to their death. Molly felt their terror as though it were her own.

She felt her shoulder moving, then she heard her mother's voice.

'Wake up, Molly,' her mother said. 'Breakfast is ready.'

Molly sat up, shaking and sweating.

'Are you sick, honey?' her mother said, touching her forehead.

'No, Mum,' Molly cried. 'I just had a terrible nightmare.'

'You poor thing,' her mother said. 'It's over now, honey. Come and have some breakfast.'

Molly wiped her face, then followed her mother to the kitchen table. Her father was there, chatting with Yosia. Both were drinking coffee.

Yosia looked at Molly and laughed.

'Sleepyhead,' he said.

'Mm,' said Molly, pulling a chair away from the table.

For a moment, she felt so small she might need a ladder to reach the seat.

'Am I awake?' she whispered.

'Yes, honey,' her mother replied.

Molly stared through the clear and empty glass in front of her, noticing the morning light break across its surface. Lost in her own world, somewhere between sleep and wakefulness, she was only vaguely aware of her mother reaching around her to put something on the table. But it was not until her mother nudged her that Molly noticed the large serving plate filled with sausages and thick slices of ham. Without warning, she burst into tears.

'What's up?' her father asked, reaching toward her.

'Those poor animals!' Molly shouted.

She ran down the hallway sobbing, then threw herself onto her bed. A few moments later, she heard a gentle tapping on her bedroom door, but she was still crying too much to answer.

Yosia entered.

'Hi,' he whispered.

Molly did not answer, but Yosia stepped inside and sat on the floor.

'I understand your feelings,' he said, leaning against the wall.

Molly blew her nose, then stared at him.

He smiled sadly.

'Some creatures on Earth have more power than others,' he said.

'It's not fair,' Molly sniffed.

'No, it's not,' Yosia agreed.

Molly dried her eyes with the sleeve of her pyjamas.

'Do *you* eat animals?' she asked.

'Not anymore,' Yosia replied, shaking his head. 'But I did when I was a young man.'

Molly screwed up her face, squeezing the last drops of tears from her eyes.

'I was born in a village where the men hunted animals to eat,' Yosia continued.

'What animals did you hunt?' Molly asked.

'Mostly tree kangaroos,' Yosia replied.

Molly remembered the lovely faces of the tree kangaroos she had seen during the previous days, and she burst into tears again. Soon, she was sobbing so deeply, she could hardly breathe.

'I'm sorry, Molly,' said Yosia. 'Please calm down.'

Molly's mother entered her bedroom.

'Oh honey, please take it easy,' she said, sitting on Molly's bed.

She placed her hand on Molly's back and moved it around in small circles.

'Take in a deep breath,' she said. 'That's it, honey. Now breath out slowly.'

A few moments later, Molly felt better.

'Good girl,' her mother said. 'You're okay now.'

Molly felt herself calming down.

'Do you feel better now?' Yosia asked.

Molly nodded.

'I've cleared the meat off the table,' her mother said. 'And I've made pancakes.'

Molly looked into her mother's eyes.

'I'm sorry for freaking out, Mum,' she said.

Her mother smiled.

'There's nothing to be sorry for, Molly,' she replied. 'You're allowed to have these feelings.'

Molly nodded again.

'Come on,' her mother said. 'Let's have breakfast.'

22

MRS. CALTHORPE'S PHONE

Molly tapped on the back door of Michael's house.

'Come in, Molly!' Mrs. Calthorpe called out.

As soon as Molly opened the door, she saw Mrs. Calthorpe sitting at her dining table behind her laptop. Beside her was Jimbo, leaning back in his chair. His head was tilted back, and he was glaring out Molly. His long-twisted nose hovered above his sneering mouth and his fingers tapped the top of the table as though he was daring Molly to come any closer.

Molly felt her heart sink, her gut clench, and her legs wobble.

'Grab a seat, Molly,' said Mrs. Calthorpe glancing over the top of her laptop screen.

Molly smiled at the woman then sat down. On the edge of her seat. As far from Jimbo as she could.

'Michael!' Mrs. Calthorpe shouted.

'Yeah?' Michael hollered back.

'Molly's here to see you!'

'Righto!'

Molly did not want to look at Jimbo, but she could feel his hateful eyes upon her. And from the edge of her vision, she could see his fingers still tapping the surface of the table.

'Stop that!' Mrs. Calthorpe hissed, placing her hand over Jimbo's.

When Molly saw the woman touch Jimbo's hand, she had a thought: *what if they are having a secret affair?* The thought was so strong, but so horrible, she had to force it out of her mind.

'Michael!' Mrs. Calthorpe hollered again.

'I'm coming!' Michael shouted.

Molly heard something thump against the floor. She imagined it might be Michael falling over as he tried to put on his shoes. Or bumping into something. For a moment, she felt a giggle coming on, but Jimbo's presence sent it back from where it had come.

'Oh, Michael!' Mrs. Calthorpe muttered, standing up.

Molly heard her stomp down the hallway.

'It's rude to keep people waiting!' Mrs. Calthorpe shouted.

Molly heard the *bing!* sound of a message arriving on Mrs. Calthorpe's laptop and her phone, almost in the same second. She glanced across the table and saw Jimbo looking sideways at the woman's computer. Then his eyes dropped to the surface of the table where Mrs. Calthorpe's phone lay. Molly knew he was snooping on Mrs. Calthorpe's work. Then suddenly she realized that might be why he had accused her of doing the same, when he had cornered her in the hospital a few days earlier.

'Have you recovered from your stay in hospital, Jimbo?' she asked.

Jimbo glared at her, his sneer growing larger.

'Honestly, that boy must have been a snail in his last life,' said Mrs. Calthorpe, blustering back to the table.

Jimbo scoffed then gazed at Mrs. Calthorpe. The sneer left his face and his dull eyes roamed around her face.

'Do you need anything else from me, Philippa?' he asked.

Mrs. Calthorpe looked up from her laptop, then sighed.

'Um, no. Thank you, Jimbo,' she replied, her tone softening and her cheeks turning pink.

Molly's gut clenched and a wave of nausea moved up to the back of her throat. Jimbo stood up and attempted to lift the top of jeans over his enormous gut, but they slid down.

'See you later, then, Philippa,' he said.

'Bye for now,' she replied, keeping her eyes on her laptop.

Jimbo walked past Molly to get to the door.

The man is vile Molly heard her own voice say inside her mind so loud that, for a moment, she was terrified she might have said it out loud.

She watched Mrs. Calthorpe's grey eyebrows pointing at each other as she continued to read something on her laptop. Then, without warning, the woman uttered a swear word so shocking, Molly swiveled in her seat, turning her back on the woman.

'Sorry for my language,' Mrs. Calthorpe whispered.

Molly did not respond because she knew there was no point. The woman's attention had already been reabsorbed by whatever she was reading. Instead, Molly gazed at the bright yellow hard hat sitting on the table and the dark blue overalls crumpled on a chair. The word 'manager' was printed across the back in bright white letters. Under better circumstances, Molly knew she would have enjoyed asking Mrs. Calthorpe what it was like to be the big boss of the mine.

But not today.

Mrs. Calthorpe's phone rang. When she picked it up, Molly saw the back of the object. It was bright yellow with pictures of blue butterflies all over it. It seemed sweet, playful, and innocent. Nothing like Mrs. Calthorpe.

Michael stepped into the kitchen, tucking his T-shirt into the top of his pants.

'Hey,' he said.

'Hey!' said Molly. 'I've got something really cool to show you.'

23

THE MAGIC UNDERGROUND

Molly led Michael to the place in her garden where she knew the magic tree stood.

'I have to tell you something,' she whispered.

'What?'

'Last night, Adali showed me how she makes the shield visible before she flies through it.'

'Really?' said Michael, sounding doubtful.

'Yes,' Molly replied, feeling excited. 'She somehow slowed down time. Everything moved so slow I could see every beat of her wings.'

'Really?' Michael said, again.

Molly nodded.

'Adali glowed, just like the magic tree glowed,' she continued. 'And when she got closer to the tree, the shield glowed, too. That's how I saw it.'

Michael frowned.

'Are you saying you actually *saw* the invisible shield?' he asked.

'Yes!' Molly replied.

'What did it look like?' he asked.

'It was almost transparent, but not quite,' Molly explained. 'It seemed to be made from a thick, clear gel that was constantly moving around the tree. It was a real, living, breathing organism. Just like the wall around the dome.'

Michael frowned, then scratched his forehead.

'It sounds like you saw electromagnetic radiation,' he said.

'Really?' said Molly.

Michael nodded.

'All objects in existence, living and nonliving, emit EMR,' he explained.

'What's EMR?' Molly asked.

Michael rolled his eyes.

'Electromagnetic radiation,' he replied. 'It's everywhere but we don't see it because its light waves are too short for our brains to perceive.'

'So, why did I see it?' Molly asked. 'And Yosia saw it, too.'

Michael scratched his head.

'You must have seen something different from normal EMR,' he said.

'How?' Molly asked.

'I don't know,' Michael replied. 'What did Yosia say about it?'

'Nothing much,' Molly replied. 'He just told me Adali had given me the demonstration to answer my question about how she flies through the shield.'

'What happened next?' Michael asked.

'Nothing,' Molly replied. 'Adali went to sleep then Yosia carried her into his hut.'

'I have an idea,' said Michael. 'Let's try to enter the shield around the tree the same way we entered the wall around the dome.'

'Okay,' said Molly.

'But let's do it from over here,' said Michael, walking to the far side of the tree.

Molly followed him.

'It's very dark here,' she said. 'We're in full shadow.'

'Exactly!' said Michael. 'We don't want anyone to see us, do we?'

'Okay then. Stand behind me and put your hands on my shoulders,' Molly said.

Michael shuffled behind Molly. Then Molly closed her eyes and took in a deep breath. The scent of the jasmine flower further down the garden wafted around her face, and the *click-clack* of the insects sounded further away than usual. She stretched her arms forward and opened her hands as wide as she could. Slowly, she stepped forward.

'I feel it now,' she whispered.

She moved her hands around until she found an indentation in the surface of the shield.

'Got it!' she whispered.

'Molly!' her father shouted.

It gave her such a fright that she fell through the shield, taking Michael with her.

'How the—' Michael started.

He stared at his hands and feet then pressed his hands into his chest and sighed.

'Wow. So *that* happened,' he said. 'The question is - how?'

'It was much faster than I expected,' said Molly. 'Do you think Dad can see or hear us in here?'

Michael waved at Molly's father, but he did not wave back, even though he was staring in the direction they were standing.

'Isn't it beautiful?' said Molly, staring up at the glowing tree.

'It sure is,' Michael whispered.

Molly looked at the bright white flowers and the bright turquoise disc-shaped leaves from which they were growing. The trunk was bright turquoise, too, and its surface was lined and lumpy, like the bark of a mature tree. But when she slid her fingertips across the trunk, Molly felt as though she was touching Play-Doh.

'Amazing,' she whispered.

Michael pressed his thumb against the trunk.

'It's soft and rubbery,' he said.

'Look!' said Molly. 'When I press hard, my fingertips sink into the bark.'

Michael did the same thing.

'Wow,' he said, his fingers sinking to his knuckles.

'Hey, look!' said Molly. 'There's a hole in the trunk, just above this branch.'

'It must be the size of a golf ball,' said Michael, running his finger around the edge.

He peered inside.

'Hm. There's nothing there,' he said. 'Just a dark and empty space.'

'Let me see,' said Molly, bringing her face toward the hole.

'Molly!' her father shouted again.

She could see him looking for her and she felt bad for hiding from him, but exploring the magic tree was much more important.

Michael brought his finger toward the hole.

'Don't stick it in!' Molly hissed. 'You never know what—'

But Michael stuck his finger into the hole. And then he vanished.

Molly just stood here, blinking, and staring at the space where Michael had been standing. Then she pinched her cheeks to make sure she was not dreaming.

'Michael?' she whispered.

There was no answer.

Molly looked around the tree to see if it had moved Michael to the other side.

'Michael,' she said. 'This isn't funny. Where are you hiding?'

Still, there was no response from Michael. Molly felt alone and afraid. She wondered how she would explain this to Michael's parents. Yosia might help, she thought, but as soon as she opened her mouth to call him, she shut it.

'Molly!' she heard someone call.

Their voice sounded thin and stretched, as though they were calling from the other side of the Milky Way, from one of those bright stars between the swirls of turquoise and gold gas clouds.

'Is that you, Michael?' Molly whispered.

'Yes! I'm in here!' Michael called back. 'I'm inside the tree and it's awesome!'

Molly looked inside the hole above the branch, but she could not see a thing.

'This is so cool!' Michael shouted. 'Just stick your finger in the hole!'

Molly could not bring herself to do it. The thought of disappearing inside the trunk of a tree was just too weird, even for her.

'I can't!' she said. 'I can't do it!'

'Come on, Molly!' Michael called out. 'It's so beautiful in here! You will love it!'

Molly brought her finger toward the hole, then pulled away.

'Molly, please!' Michael called out.

Molly's curiosity was building. She wanted to stick her finger into the hole, on the chance that something else might happen. Something that did not involve being sucked inside the trunk of the tree.

'Molly!' her father called. 'Answer me!'

The sound of her father's angry voice made Molly panic. She felt her legs wobbling.

'Molly!' he shouted again.

Before she knew it, Molly had stuck her finger in the hole. She heard a loud *pop!* as her body was pulled forward. A second later, she was pulled down fast. So fast, she had to grip the hem of her dress to stop it from blowing over her head.

'Help!' she cried.

Something took hold of her waist, slowing her fall. She glided down gently. A moment later, her feet touched the ground, and she found herself standing beside Michael.

'You made it!' he said, smiling. 'Isn't this amazing?'

Molly found herself standing in the strangest place she had ever seen.

24

THE MYCELIUM NETWORK

Molly was surrounded by the color brown. But as her eyes adjusted, she saw some black wiggly lines meandering through the clumps of brown and some thinner white lines wrapped around them. And there was a familiar earthy scent that she loved.

'Tree roots,' she whispered.

'Yep,' said Michael.

'Are we under the ground?' she asked.

'Yep,' Michael replied.

There was only one source of light, and it was the thin white lines. Molly saw lots of them, branching away in all directions, it seemed.

'Fungi!' she said.

'Yep,' said Michael. 'Welcome to the mycelium network - the underworld of fungi!'

Molly stared at the mycelium, noticing how large some of the white fibers were. One, directly above her head, was almost as wide as her face.

'Have we shrunk?' she asked.

She was joking, and she expected Michael to laugh at her. But he didn't.

'Yep,' he said.

Before Molly knew it, her heart was pounding, and her legs were wobbling. She felt sweaty all over, and her throat felt tight, as though she was going to scream. The faces of her mother, father, Yosia and Adaline flashed through her mind, and she felt herself reaching for them.

'Wha—' she stammered.

'Relax,' said Michael. 'It's only temporary.'

'You don't know that!' Molly shrieked.

'It's okay, Molly,' said Michael. 'We'll get home again, don't worry.'

'Don't worry!' Molly shrieked again. 'We are the size of ants, and you're saying *don't worry?*'

Michael took a step back, keeping his eyes on Molly.

'You're being weird,' he said. 'Usually, it's *you* who wants these crazy adventures.'

'Michael, we need help!' Molly shrieked. 'Call Adali now!'

Michael frowned.

'Do you mean Adali, the bird?' he asked.

'Yes!' said Molly.

Michael scoffed.

'What's the bird going to do?' he asked. 'Other than eat us, of course.'

Molly gasped. The thought of being eaten by her friend Adali, was too much.

'What shall we do?' she cried.

Michael shrugged, then gave her a sad smile.

'Follow the mycelium network,' he replied. 'That's what it wants us to do.'

Molly stared at the boy, struggling to understand him.

'Do you honestly think the network is *speaking* to you?' she asked.

Michael nodded.

'It has been ever since I arrived here,' he replied. 'Can't you hear it?'

Molly shook her head.

'Come on,' said Michael, waving Molly toward him.

Molly could not think of anything else to do, so she stepped onto the thick strand of glowing white mycelium. It vibrated, then moved forward, forging a tunnel through the dark soil.

25

THE AMAZING LIFE OF FUNGI

Traveling on the mycelium network was both amazing and weird, Molly decided. Its luminous glow was beautiful, and a welcome relief from the endless piles of dark brown dirt and rocks. But she could not forget that she was so small, she might be killed by an insect at any moment. The thought was too horrific to entertain, so she tried to steer away from it, but it continued to haunt her. She also thought it strange that Michael was not worried.

'Did you eat or drink anything down here while you were waiting for me?' she asked.

'No,' Michael scoffed. 'What would there be to eat or drink down here?'

Molly knew the only source of life would be the bacteria and water molecules from the soil. The mycelium network would be transporting them to the mushrooms and trees above the surface. She thought about the amazing life of fungi.

'Did you know that the largest living thing on this

planet is a fungus?' she said. 'It's called Armillaria somethingorother.'

'Tell me about it,' said Michael.

'It lives in Oregon, in North America, and it's almost six kilometers wide,' Molly replied.

'That's big,' said Michael.

'It's so big that the aerial photographs show it as a huge yellow patch amidst the green forest,' Molly explained. 'And some of the mushrooms that grow from it are even taller than adults.'

'Awesome,' said Michael. 'Here's another fun fact - fungi helped us win World War One.'

'Us?' Molly echoed. 'Do you mean us Australians?'

'No, our allies,' Michael replied. 'The British, actually. Whenever their soldiers were injured, they would slap a piece of moldy bread onto the wound to prevent infection.'

'That doesn't make much sense,' said Molly.

'It makes perfect sense,' Michael replied. 'When you think about the fact that penicillin is made from fungi, and penicillin kills bacteria, it makes perfect sense.'

'Yeah, I guess,' Molly agreed. 'All types of fungi are amazing.'

'Fungi will attack and conquer bacteria every time the two are put together,' Michael said.

Molly wondered what bacteria and fungi would look like under a microscope. All those shapes and colors would be fascinating, she imagined. Then something else popped into her mind.

'Actually, it still doesn't make absolute sense,' she said.

'What's your problem now?' Michael asked.

'Well, I'm pretty sure that lichen is a cross between fungi and alga. As you know, alga is a type of bacteria,' Molly argued.

'Hm,' said Michael. 'I don't know what to say to that.'

'I just remembered something else,' Molly continued. 'When we were in the cave a few days ago, your father said something about copper sulfate being used in medicines to kill fungi *and* bacteria.'

'True,' said Michael.

'So that might change things down here,' Molly said.

'What do you mean?' Michael asked.

'If we go near the mine, this mycelium network will probably disappear,' Molly replied.

'I hadn't thought of that,' said Michael.

An immense pile of dirt fell into the center of the tunnel, completely covering the boy. All Molly could see of him were his hazel eyes and a thin circle of white skin around them. That was funny enough, but when Michael opened his mouth, a pile of dirt fell out. This made Molly laugh so much, she failed to notice another strand of mycelium slide under her feet. She got such a surprised, she lost her balance and landed on her butt.

'Ha! Who looks stupid now?' said Michael.

'Look at that!' said Molly, pointing to the mycelium strand.

It was ploughing through the soil as easily as a jet ski moves through water.

'It's forming another tunnel,' said Michael.

'It's also listening to us,' Molly said, placing her hands on the glowing strand.

'Gon on then,' said Michael. 'Talk to it.'

Molly giggled, then brought her mouth closer to the mycelium strand.

'Hello, we know you are conscious,' she said. 'What do you want to tell us?'

Michael scoffed.

'What a dork,' he said.

The tunnel opened wider, and the strand forged ahead in a downward direction.

'We have our answer,' said Molly, bending her knees, as though surfing a giant wave.

And as they descended, she noticed the soil getter darker with every second. The temperature was increasing, too. She wanted to wipe the sweat from her face because it was starting to itch, but she did not dare let go of the moving strand of mycelium.

'This is like Journey to the Center of the Earth!' she shouted. 'Did you ever read that book?'

'Are you kidding?' Michael called back. 'That's one of my favorite books of all time!'

Molly gave the strand a squeeze, enjoying the springy sensation between her hands.

'I reckon this thing must be filled with a thick gel,' she called out.

'Yeah, I do, too,' Michael replied. 'I reckon it's the same stuff you saw in the shield around the magic tree. And in the wall of the dome.'

'Me too!' Molly shouted. 'And I'll bet the entire thing is one massive organism with billions of brain cells talking to each other at the speed of light!'

'Now you're talking!' said Michael. 'It's like a massive, organic supercomputer!'

'Ha, ha!' Molly shouted, still clinging to the moving strand. 'But I reckon it feels more like another person. A person who doesn't speak.'

'Have you noticed the soil is changing again?' Michael asked.

'Yes, it's a pale grey color now,' Molly replied. 'And it's less dense.'

Michael reached toward the wall of the tunnel and grabbed a clump of pale grey soil. Immediately, it crumbled and slipped through his fingers like fine dust.

'There's not much in it, is there?' said Molly.

'Nope,' Michael replied.

But the mycelium did not care. It just kept moving.

26

DOWN A TUNNEL

Molly was not sure how long she and Michael had been traveling on the mycelium strand. Neither one had spoken for a while, and that was fine with her. She did not mind the silence. Her mind felt perfectly calm and happy. She was no longer concerned about her size, or her destination, she was just enjoying the adventure. But when a strange rumbling sensation moved through the soil and caused a shudder under her feet, she felt mildly curious.

'What was that?' she asked.

Before Michael could reply, the same thing happened again.

'Oh no,' he said, turning around to look at her.

A third rumbling came, then even more soil fell from the walls of the tunnel.

'What's happening?' Molly asked.

'It must be an earthquake,' Michael replied, looking up.

'Oh, no,' said Molly.

'Hang on a minute,' said Michael, removing his backpack.

He rummaged through the bag for a moment, then retrieved a small round compass.

'I don't know how accurate this will be down here,' he said.

'How do you make sense of that thing?' Molly asked, frowning at the old, cracked object.

Michael winked at Molly.

'It's pretty simple, really,' he replied. 'It's telling me we're moving in a northwest direction, and the mine is located northwest of our house, therefore we are moving toward the mine.'

'Okay,' said Molly. 'If you say so.'

A fourth tremor disturbed the soil, making the mycelium lurch forward so suddenly it threw Molly and Michael down the tunnel. They fell for several seconds. Long enough for Molly to think about opening her hands and grabbing Michael's backpack if she needed to land on it. She also saw the walls of the tunnel expanding, causing more of the grey dirt to spiral around her and Michael. Where they were going, and when they might stop, she had no idea.

Eventually, Molly landed on Michael's leg, and he howled in pain.

'Sorry,' she cried, sliding off him.

She stood up, shook the dirt off her dress, and looked around.

'No wonder it hurt,' she said. 'We've landed on a rock.'

Michael gripped his leg, wincing in pain.

'Oh, no,' said Molly, thinking of Michael's father and his recent knee injury.

'I'll be okay,' Michael groaned.

Molly felt herself silently praying for Michael to recover, because she knew there would be no way of rescuing him. Even if she could find her way out of this strange place, and call for help, no one would hear her voice because she was only the size of an ant. There was only one solution, she knew, and it was for her and Michael to survive this bizarre underground experience and return to normal.

'I'm sure my eyes are adjusting to the darkness in this tunnel,' she said.

'Yeah, me too,' said Michael. 'But the mycelium strand is still helping us.'

'What do you mean?' Molly asked.

'It's up there, Molly, look,' said Michael, pointing to the top of the tunnel.

When Molly looked, she saw the strand dangling into the tunnel.

'If only it was long enough to grab hold of,' she said.

For now, her priority was to get Michael mobile again.

'Are you able to stand?' she asked.

Michael scrambled to his feet, leaning on Molly's shoulder.

'How do you feel?' she asked.

'Not bad, considering the situation,' Michael replied.

He tried to laugh but made a sound more like a short whimper. Molly wrapped her arm around his enormous waist and was just about to suggest they take a step forward, when she realized she did not know which way forward was. In all directions, she saw nothing but rocks and dirt. Until one huge mound of dirt moved aside.

'There's another mycelium strand coming through,' she said. 'Maybe it will pull us back up.'

But as the pile of dirt moved a bit more, Molly was surprised she could not see the glow of the mycelium network. There was something else poking through the dirt. It was a reddish-brown color.

'Oh, no!' Michael shrieked. 'It's a worm!'

Molly could not believe what Michael was saying. The thought of dealing with an earthworm while she was only the size of an ant was not a situation she had ever imagined. And yet, the worm was slithering through the dirt, straight toward Michael.

'Ergh,' he groaned.

When it stopped only centimeters from Michael's face, Molly feared he might scream. Instead, he seemed to freeze with terror. Molly stared at the thing.

'Wow,' she whispered. 'I didn't know they had hair on their faces.'

'Do you call that a face?' Michael shrieked.

Michael was right - the worm did not have a face. It just had an end that was covered with tiny hairs. Molly remembered reading somewhere that the hairs help it to sense movement.

'If we remain perfectly still, it might move on,' she whispered.

'Um, bad news, Molly,' said Michael. 'There's another one coming through.'

Molly watched another worm slither forward. And then another. And then a third. Then she remembered earthworms live in herds and make collective decisions through touch. All those hairs on their heads would be sending messages to the other worms in the herd. They would be discussing the potential food source in front of them. She just hoped she and Michael would not be on their menu.

She could only turn her head enough to stare at Michael. He seemed to have turned a grey-green color. Molly knew he would have felt incredibly vulnerable, because the pain in his leg would be stopping him from running. But then she realized there would be no point in running because they would not be able to see where they were going. And wherever they went, the worms could go faster.

Another three worms slithered into the space.

'Oh, geez,' said Michael.

The worms were all bumping heads. Some became entwined, too, like long strings of cooked spaghetti. It was an unwelcome thought that Molly had to force out of her mind because it was making her feel even sicker.

'They really are hideous,' she hissed.

Michael pointed up.

'The tunnel we fell through is still there,' he said.

Molly looked up the tunnel and saw the dim glow from the mycelium strand above.

'Thank goodness it's still there,' she whispered. 'If only we could climb back up without these creepy worms sensing us.'

Michael shook his head.

'It's still not safe to move,' he whispered.

Molly looked at the herd of worms again. Some seemed to have lost interest in whatever they had been discussing, because they had stopped bumping heads. Some had even lowered their heads and one was wriggling away. But one worm, it seemed, was very interested in her presence. It wriggled right up to her until it was only millimeters from her face.

It was so ugly, she did not want to look at it. But she could not help it. As it moved its head, she saw something that vaguely resembled a mouth. When it opened, she could see it was just a hairy, slimy hole. And inside the hole was a small brown lump. Molly thought it might be a piece of dirt or the poop from an insect. She did not want to know.

'I can't take it anymore,' she cried, pressing her face into Michael's shoulder.

She decided she would keep her eyes closed, and she promised herself she would not open them again. Even if the worm started to eat her. Michael was making a sound she had never heard before. It sounded like a mix between sobbing and vomiting. She did not know, exactly.

She felt another tremor then saw mounds of soil fall away, taking the worms with it.

'Oh, thank goodness,' she gasped.

Finally, Molly could see and feel much more space around her. There was even a rock for her and Michael to sit on, so they did. She stared up at the top of the tunnel.

The mycelium strand above them was still glowing, like the light on a taxicab. Michael looked up, too.

'That thing actually threw us down here on purpose, didn't it?' he said.

'It certainly feels that way,' Molly replied.

Michael rubbed his face, then gasped.

'Can you see that crack between those rocks ahead?' he asked.

Molly could see the crack, but only because of the warm light peeping through.

'Yes!' she said, wiping the sweat and tears from her face. 'Let's check it out.'

When they arrived at the crack, Molly pressed her cheeks against the warm rocks. She felt a wave of relief wash over her because she finally knew what she was looking at. The huge space - filled with enormous orange haul trucks and yellow excavation cranes - was the place she had been standing in a few days earlier when Mr. Calthorpe's knee had broken. And the men on the far side of the space were shoveling rocks onto the flat black tray, just as they had done before.

'It's the mine, all right!' Michael shouted.

'It might be grand in there, but it's horrible,' said Molly.

'What do you mean?'

Molly scrunched up her face, trying to think of the right words to explain how she felt.

'Those poor people,' she said. 'They're doing the same things they did yesterday and the day before that and the day before that. And those machines are so noisy. And there's so much dust in there and they're using horrible chemicals to extract the copper from the ore.'

Michael shrugged.

'That's what mining is,' he said. 'What else are they supposed to do?'

'They're polluting the water and the land!' said Molly. 'It's all ... just ... wrong.'

Michael grunted.

'It's wrong!' Molly shouted. 'Everything they're doing in there is upsetting the earth out here!'

Before Molly could say anything more, something wrapped around her ankle and lifted her so fast she had no time to make sense of what was happening. Below her, a tornado of dirt spiraled downward. At its center, she could see Michael's feet as he was being pulled up after her.

'Michael!' she shouted. 'Call Adali!'

Molly did not hear a response from Michael, so she called out again.

'Call Adali!' she called out again.

This time, a pile of soil landed on her tongue. She spat it out, coughed, and then shut her mouth. She also pressed her chin into her chest to stop the soil from flying up her nose, but she soon felt she was running out of air. Her chest was starting to collapse, she was feeling dizzy, and her head was starting to pound. *This is the end,* she heard herself say inside her mind. *I'll never see my parents again.*

But through her half-opened eyes, Molly could see the surrounding soil was getting darker, and she dared to hope the mycelium was bringing her to the surface. *Any second now,* she told herself. *It will fling me through the surface into the fresh air.* But the mycelium did not do that. Instead, it dragged her sideways, just below the surface.

Molly caught tiny glimpses of sunlight peeping through the soil, and she gulped some fresh air. The dry leaves, and other bits of rotting organic material, smelled terrible as the mycelium fiber moved beneath them. The awful journey went on for so long, she gave up. She no longer hoped for rescue or relief. She just closed her eyes and breathed in deep and slow, allowing her limbs to relax and stretch as far as they could.

Inside her mind, Molly saw the lovely faces of her mother and father. Then she saw the faces of Yosia and Adaline and Michael. She hoped Mr. Calthorpe's knee would heal soon, and that Mrs. Calthorpe might enjoy planting some vegetables in her garden again. Finally, she thought about her beloved black cat, Kiki, waiting for her at home in Australia. She imagined herself wrapping her arms around Kiki's lovely round body and holding her so close, she would feel the vibrations of the cat's purr through her entire body. *I love you, Kiki,* she heard herself think. *See you in heaven.*

A moment later, she landed with a *thud!* Then Michael landed beside her.

27

ASK POLITELY

Molly lay still, hoping she was not broken. But every part of her body hurt. And her mouth was as dry as a roll of sandpaper.

'Are you okay?' Michael croaked.

'I think so,' Molly whispered. 'This must be what it feels like to survive a tornado.'

Her eyes were the only part of her body moving. She could see she was still under the ground, surrounded by dark brown dirt. She pressed her palms into the ground and squeezed two clumps of warm, moist soil between her fingers.

'Where are we now?' she whispered.

'Dunno,' Michael replied. 'But my back is killing me.'

She sat up and leaned over him.

'No wonder,' she said. 'You've landed on your backpack.'

Slowly, she slipped the straps off Michael's shoulders. Even more slowly, he sat up.

'Can you roll your shoulders?' she asked.

Michael rolled his shoulders, then moved his head from side to side.

'It's still glued on,' he said. 'That's a good start.'

Michael pressed his fists into the center of his back and stretched. Molly rolled onto her side and curled into a ball, unwilling to sit up fully. She closed her eyes and exhaled deeply. Through the soil, she saw the dim glow of a strand of mycelium. She brushed the soil away, revealing the bright white fiber, then she wrapped her fingers around it.

'Please be kind to us,' she whispered. 'We mean you no harm.'

The mycelium strand wriggled closer to Molly. Slowly and gently, it wrapped itself around her waist and lifted her to a standing position. Her body ached. She felt weak and dizzy, but somehow, she knew she could stand by herself.

'Okay,' she said, touching the mycelium. 'Please let me go, now.'

The mycelium did as she asked.

Michael opened his water bottle, took a sip, then handed it to Molly. From the first drop on her tongue, she knew she needed it and she guzzled.

'Steady on,' said Michael, taking the bottle away.

He placed a power bar in Molly's empty hands, then watched with raised eyebrows as she ripped the wrapper off the bar and sunk her teeth into the firm chocolate flavored lump. Molly knew she was gorging like a person who had not eaten in days, but Michael was worse. He made the most awful slurping and chomping sounds as he ate his power bar.

Molly stared at the strand of mycelium.

'Please take us home,' she cried.

The mycelium glowed even more brightly and then made a happy *ting!* sound.

'All aboard!' Michael shouted, stepping onto the strand.

Molly stood behind him, feeling the mycelium's warmth traveling through the soles of her feet, up her legs, waist, chest, neck, face, and arms. Her entire body was receiving the network's healing vibes, and for that, she was grateful. Then it moved up at such a steep incline, Molly and Michael had to wrap their arms and legs around it to ensure they did not slide off.

'With a bit of luck, it's taking us to the surface,' said Michael.

Molly could hear the mycelium moving through the soil and debris. To her tiny ears, it sounded like a load of gravel sliding off the back of a truck. She closed her eyes, pressed her face against the strand, and inhaled the earthy scent she loved so much. Then, with one last tug, the mycelium pulled her and Michael through the surface of the soil.

28

WHERE ARE WE NOW?

Molly gasped with relief. She rubbed her hands over her face and smoothed her hair. Then she leaned against something soft. It was a creamy pinkish color, and it smelled lovely, like one of her mother's dinners. She pressed her hand into it, staring at the little imprints that her fingers left on the surface.

'Springy,' she said.

'There's a reason for that,' said Michael, looking up.

Molly looked up at the dome-shaped ceiling. With folds that sprung from the center then drooped to the outer edge, it was like something from a theme park or a —

'Are we in an art gallery?' she asked.

'For goodness' sake!' said Michael. 'We're standing under a mushroom!'

'What?' Molly said, stepping back.

She looked around and saw several mushroom-shaped structures. Some were taller than others, but they were all the same shape. Her mind flashed back to the last time she had washed and sliced mushrooms in the kitchen with her mother. She had fried them in butter and garlic until they had turned golden brown. Then she had piled them onto toast, sprinkled crumbs of feta cheese over the top and handed the plate to her mother. When she mother had taken the first bite then said: 'Oh, yeah, that's good,' Molly's heart had swelled with pride.

'We missed lunch,' said Molly, her eyes filling with tears. 'What will our parents be thinking?'

Michael sighed, then pushed his hair off his forehead.

'We're going to get in trouble again, for sure,' he said.

'If we ever get home, ' Molly cried.

'Well, let's make a start,' said the boy.

Molly followed him around the mushroom stalks. The green moss beneath their feet was so soft and thick, her feet sunk into it with every step. The air was warm and damp, and there was a gentle buzzing in the background. At first, Molly thought the sound was coming from behind her, then it seemed to come from another direction. And the volume seemed to be going up and down.

'What is that?' she said.

Michael glanced over his shoulder, then grabbed Molly's hand.

'Run!' he shouted.

Molly glanced behind her just in time to see a fly, about the same size as her, zooming toward her. She recognized it as the same species she had seen when she had grown mushrooms in her shed in Australia. She had killed them by sprinkling a fine powder onto the surrounding soil. This fly, it seemed, was seeking revenge.

From both sides of the insect's head bulged two compound eyes, each covered with what looked like hundreds of curvy TV screens. The sound of its wings suddenly reminded Molly of the electric drill her dentist had used to remove one of her teeth the previous year. And there was something about the way the fly held up its front legs that made her feel it might be looking forward to eating her.

It took every bit of energy in every cell of Molly's exhausted body to keep running. But with every step, she was finding it easier. She was lifting her feet faster and taking bigger steps. Soon she was bouncing across the mossy ground. And the green blur of plants around her seemed to be getter smaller.

'We're getting bigger!' she shrieked.

Michael gripped her hand even tighter as they stepped onto a shiny grey path. *Wet concrete,* Molly realized, as she slipped. She landed on her side, but Michael did not stop, nor did he let go of her hand.

'Hold your breath!' he shouted as he dragged her headfirst into a pond.

Molly's skin prickled with the shock of falling below the surface of the water. But she opened her eyes, and saw Michael facing her, treading water. His wooly hair wafted upward like a clump of seaweed, making him look at home, like *Shrek* in his swamp.

When their faces broke through the surface, they were both laughing.

'At least we got all that dirt washed off!' said Molly, pushing her wet hair off her face.

'Yeah! And we're normal size again!' Michael shouted, punching the air.

'Thank goodness!' Molly squealed, flicking some water into the boy's face. 'It must be because we're away from the mycelium network.'

'Probably,' Michael replied, looking around. 'Do you realize we're in the dome?'

'Huh?'

Molly stared up at the familiar grand ceiling.

'Oh my gosh, we are, too,' she said.

Michael swam to the edge of the pond, then climbed out. His jeans and T-shirt stuck to his round body. And his backpack, somehow still secured to his torso, released a river of murky green water.

'You should take it off,' Molly called out, laughing.

'Yeah,' he replied, slipping the bag off his shoulders.

'At least we can check this place out,' said Molly.

She swam to the center of the pond, where a huddle of pink water lilies stood straight and tall. Their pointy petals wide open so she squeezed one between her thumb and forefinger.

'It's so smooth,' she said.

She remembered a holiday she once had in Bali. The waterlilies had been everywhere, and her mother had taken hundreds of photos of them.

'We must have been gone for hours,' said Molly.

'Yeah, I'd say so,' Michael replied. 'I wish I'd worn my watch today.'

'Ah, it's just as well you didn't,' Molly replied, swimming toward him. 'It would—Ergh!' she shouted, feeling something slimy on her elbow.

She lifted her arm out of the water, horrified to see a frog's mouth wrapped around her elbow. The creature was brown with white dots all over its back. Its eyes looked dull and cloudy, like a person who was blind from cataracts.

'What's it doing?' she shrieked.

'Dunno,' said Michael. 'Frogs don't normally behave like that.'

Molly shook her arm, but the frog did not let go. It just hung there, like a giant skin tag.

'Oh, yuk, I think there's another one on my leg,' she squealed. 'Help me!'

Michael jumped back into the pond then waded toward Molly. He peeled the frog off her elbow and threw it to the far side of the pond. Then he pulled another off her leg. Then a third frog attached itself to his shoulder. Molly pulled it off him.

'We have to get out of here,' she said.

She saw another frog leap out of the water and latch onto Michael's elbow.

'Geez, this could go on forever,' he groaned, peeling it off. 'Let's just get out.'

They swam to the edge of the pond, then pressed their hands into the edge of a rock and pulled themselves out. Molly felt another frog on her calf.

'Oh, yuk!' she shrieked, peeling it away.

She threw it as hard as she could to the far side of the pond, noticing how dead it seemed.

'They're like zombie frogs,' she said.

Michael laughed out loud.

'I think Yosia would call them *unnatural*,' he said.

'Agreed,' said Molly. 'Yet another bizarre creation in the name of science.'

'Or, perhaps, an unintended byproduct of whatever they are doing in here,' Michael said.

Molly squeezed the green water from her dress and hair and watched it pool in the little dents on the surface of the stone. Then she noticed the silence. Michael was silently gazing ahead at the many clusters of strange plants.

'You know, for a lazy oaf, you can run fast when you have to,' she said, laughing.

'Hey!' said Michael, scowling. 'Who are you calling lazy?'

Molly looked at the boy, surprised he did not think of himself as lazy, but also surprised by her own rudeness.

'I'm sorry,' she said. 'I didn't mean to offend you.'

'It's okay,' said Michael. 'I suppose I am lazy. I just don't see the point in exerting myself when I don't have to.'

She also remembered Michael had seemed bored and grumpy when she had first met him. He had confessed to her he had been lonely, too, and that was why he had hunted butterflies and pinned them to his bedroom wall. She remembered thinking of him as the most evil person on the planet. But she knew better now.

'Do you still have those binoculars?' she asked.

'Yep,' Michael replied, pulling them from his backpack.

Molly snatched the lenses from the boy's hands and placed them over her eyes.

'What is it about those binoculars that makes you rude and snatchy?' said Michael.

'Sorry,' Molly said, squinting through the drops of water on the lenses.

She stared at the regular pattern of steel dots on the ceiling of the dome, recognizing them from the last time she and Michael had been inside the dome.

'That's the irrigation system, all right,' she said. 'It looks the same as before.'

'Yep,' said Michael, taking the binoculars from Molly's eager hands. 'And it's just as quiet now, as it was last time. I'm exhausted, Molly. I'd like to sit here for a while.'

'Sounds good to me,' said Molly.

She stretched her legs out in front of her, then leaned back and closed her eyes, enjoying the silence. But only for a moment. Then her curiosity sparked again.

'So, before you came to PNG, where did you live?' she asked.

Michael gasped, as though Molly had just woken him from a nap.

'Sorry,' she said. 'We don't have to talk if you don't want to.'

'Werribee,' Michael replied, rubbing his eyes. 'On the south-west coast of Melbourne.'

'What's it like?' Molly asked.

Michael shrugged his shoulders.

'Okay, I suppose,' he replied. 'Our house was near the Werribee River, so we used to go fishing there. We caught a lot of bream, which cook up nice on the barbie.'

'Are you an only child, like me?' Molly asked.

Michael paused for a moment, then looked down at the pond.

'Sort of,' he replied. 'Yeah. I am now.'

'Are you sure?' Molly asked.

Michael cleared his throat.

'I had an older sister, but she died when I was a baby,' he whispered.

'Oh. I'm so sorry,' said Molly.

'Well, it's not as though I knew her,' Michael said. 'But I sort of feel like I know her because Mum and Dad talk about her a lot. Especially on her birthday. And at Christmas time.'

Molly tried to imagine what that might feel like.

'It must be like living with a ghost,' she said.

Michael wiped a trickle of tears off his cheek.

'Sometimes I wish she'd never been born,' he said. 'Then I'd never see Mum and Dad crying. But I feel terrible for saying that. Do you think I'm terrible?'

'No!' Molly replied. 'Your feelings are perfectly understandable.'

She gazed at the family of pink waterlilies in the center of the pond, apparently untouched by the creepy frogs. And frogs, she figured, must have stopped moving because the surface of the pod was completely flat. It seemed dead.

'My sister drowned in the sea,' said Michael.

Molly gasped, then imagined a small girl slipping peacefully under the surface of the ocean. No fuss. No panic. Just ... gone.

'You know how violent the rip currents can be in Australia,' Michael continued. 'Apparently I was sitting on the sand with Mum when it happened.'

'Gosh, I'm so sorry,' said Molly. 'That's awful.'

'We've never been back to the ocean since that day,' said Michael. 'Mum and Dad won't even let me go there on school excursions.'

Molly felt terrible for the boy. To never see the ocean or soak your feet in the salty water or breathe the glorious fresh air would be a tragedy. She looked at Michael, hunched over like a big sad lump, and she wanted to hug him. But as she reached toward him, she got the feeling he would not like that.

'Enough about me,' he said, sitting up. 'What about you? Where do you live?'

'Calga,' Molly replied. 'It's north of Sydney and inland a bit. The best thing about it is the Wildlife Walkabout Park.'

Michael nodded.

'The best day was when I got to cuddle a koala,' Molly continued. 'She was a young female with no babies to protect, so she didn't mind.'

'I'll bet she was nice and soft,' said Michael.

'Not as soft as you'd expect,' Molly replied. 'But it was wonderful to see her look up into my eyes and feel her little heart beating against mine.

'That's lovely,' said Michael. 'Are you in PNG for a year? Same as us?'

'Yes,' Molly replied. 'I hope it's not any longer. I miss my cat, Kiki. I really, really miss her.'

'I know how you feel,' said Michael. 'I miss my dog, Bozo.'

Molly tried to imagine what Bozo might look like, but all she saw was the furry black face of her lovely Kiki. The cat's big green eyes would stare at her for what felt like a long time, then suddenly, she would wink. That would make Molly laugh, and she would pull the cat closer for a cuddle. Then Kiki would start purring.

'I wonder what Kiki and Bozo think of us for leaving them,' she said.

Michael looked serious and thoughtful for a moment. Then he shrugged.

'They're probably not thinking of anything except their next meal,' he said.

Molly laughed.

'Speaking of food,' she said, shaking Michael's backpack.

A soggy cheese sandwich fell out.

'Oh, yuk,' said Molly. 'Even when it dries, it won't be fit for eating.'

'At least we know we can get home for dinner,' Michael said, standing up. 'Are you ready to get going again?'

'Ready as ever!' Molly replied.

29

INSIDE THE DOME

Molly's wet sandals hung from her fingers, leaving a trickle of water on the concrete path.

'Do you think it's about midday?' she asked.

'It feels like it,' Michael replied. 'But after the things we've been through, I no longer trust my own instincts.'

Molly could hear the exhaustion in Michael's voice. She did not want to pester him with boring conversation, but she did not want silence, either. It was simply too quiet inside the dome. She could not hear a single insect or bird. There was no breeze rustling through trees. It felt unnatural.

'I suppose the irrigation switches on at night,' she said.

'Yeah, probably,' Michael replied.

Molly listened to the sound of her bare feet on the concrete path.

'Do you think we're alone?' she asked.

Michael glanced at her.

'Dunno,' he said. 'It's pretty quiet in here, isn't it?'

'Mm,' said Molly, nudging him off the main path.

'What are you doing?' he said.

The narrow path was straight, unlike the others, and it led to the wall.

Molly stared at it.

'I should be able to get us through that wall,' she said. 'Then we'll wander around the sinkhole until we find the entrance to the cave.'

'Yep,' said Michael, his tone flat. 'Then we'll have a long walk up a steep incline before we exit the side of the mountain.'

'True,' Molly said. 'But after that, it will be downhill.'

Michael did not respond.

'This is the opportunity we've been hoping for,' said Molly.

But she could tell - Michael was no longer in the mood for exploring. He seemed sad. Molly wondered if it was because he had been talking about his sister's death and if that had led him to think about his father in hospital and mother's monster behaviour during the last few days. But she did not know for sure.

The only thing Molly knew was that it might be best to be quiet for a while.

She enjoyed the look of the fleshy plants on both sides of the path. The cluster to her left was about as high as her shoulders. The trunks were dark green and appeared to be fleshy in texture. Their leaves were wide and flat and bright orange. At their center was a vein of the same color, but with a neat row of bright green dots starting large and getting smaller the closer they got to the tip of the leaves.

'It's almost as though someone had taken to them with a paintbrush!' she said.

'It's really strange,' said Michael. 'Look at these!'

Molly followed Michael's gaze to the opposite side of the path. There she saw a collection of plants with brown trunks and bright pink leaves shaped like dinner bowls.

'What in the world are?' she whispered.

'And this!' said Michael, pointing to another cluster.

They were short, thick shrubs covered in berries that were red on one side and bright yellow on the other side. There were so many, Molly could barely see the dark green leaves between them.

'Gosh, this is weird,' she said. 'But I notice there's none of that turquoise color at the base of the trunks, as there was in the plants in the volcano.'

Michael stopped and stared at her.

'You're right,' he said, frowning. 'The only turquoise thing in here is that massive vine around the wall,' he added, pointing at the wall ahead.

Molly exhaled deeply.

'There must be a way of explaining how all this fits together,' she said.

Michael let out a loud groan.

'Molly, everything that's happened during the last few days has been really weird,' he said.

'I know!' Molly giggled.

Then she saw Michael's bottom lip quivering.

He opened one of his hands and used his fingers to count.

'The first one was the weird butterfly rebirth,' he said.

'Mm,' said Molly, nodding.

'The next day, we visited the mine and my dad got hurt.'

'I know,' Molly whispered, relieved Michael had finally acknowledged it.

But he was not finished.

'The day after that, we climbed down to the bottom of the volcano and saw plants and animals that simply do not exist!' he shrieked.

His mouth was quavering even more now, and his face was getting redder. Molly stepped closer to him to offer comfort. But he held up his hand, so she stepped back.

'The next day we got chased through the jungle by a cassowary that wanted to kill us, then we fell down the side of a mountain, cracked our heads on some rocks and got sunburnt. Dehydrated, we staggered over the sinkhole and discovered this invisible dome!'

Michael's face was still getting redder, and there was spit shooting out of his mouth.

'And if all of that was not enough!' he shrieked. 'You stole a flower, planted it in your garden, and a full-sized tree grew overnight.'

'Okay,' Molly said, using the same tone her parents have always used with her whenever they wanted her to stop shouting.

'Then the tree shrunk us down to the size of ants and pulled us under the ground, where a *fungus* dragged us around like we were a pair of rag dolls. And after all that, we got chased by a fly into a filthy, slimy pond!'

Molly took in a deep breath, keeping her eyes on her

friend. Eventually, his face returned to its usual color, then his shoulders slumped.

'It's okay,' Molly whispered. 'We're okay now.'

'Yes, I know we're okay now!' Michael shouted. 'But for how long?'

Molly did not know the answer to that question, but she felt it best to say something that might make Michael feel better.

'Once we get home, we'll stay there and totally chill out,' she said.

'I just want to understand what's happening!' Michael shouted, his eyes filling with tears.

'I don't know what's happening,' Molly whispered. 'I've never seen magic like this before.'

Michael rubbed his eyes so hard Molly feared he might injure them.

'There's no such thing as magic!' he shouted.

Then he gasped, flopped onto the ground, and dropped his head into his hands.

Molly sat beside him and rested her head on his shoulder.

'It's going to be okay,' she said.

But she was not so sure.

30

RUN FOR YOUR LIFE!

Molly sat on the warm concrete path, staring at the cluster of plants in front of her. They had thick brown trunks and bright green leaves. The soil was so dark; it was almost black. She knew that meant it was high in organic compounds. Which made sense, considering how meticulous this huge experiment seemed to be. She noticed a small, bright yellow ball sitting exactly half-way between two trunks. Then she saw another. And another. There were lots of them, placed at regular intervals.

'What do you suppose they are?' she asked.

Michael lifted his head from his hands and looked up.

'No, down here, on the ground,' said Molly. 'Those yellow balls.'

She watched Michael's eyes dart from one ball to another.

'They're about two meters apart, aren't they?' he said.

'What are they?' Molly asked again.

Michael shrugged.

'Probably a slow-release fertilizer for the plants,' he replied.

'I wonder what chemicals they're releasing,' said Molly.

'Probably the kind that's none of our business,' Michael replied.

Molly pulled her damp handkerchief from her pocket and wrapped it around her forefinger.

'I want to take a sample for Eddie,' she said.

'That's not a good idea,' said Michael.

But Molly had already crawled to the edge of the soil. The lower branches and tree trunks blocked out most of the sunlight, but she could still see the yellow balls.

'I'll just go as far as that first one,' she said.

As she crawled across the soil, Molly noticed the absence of the earthy scent she loved so much. This soil smelled of absolutely nothing. Just as the gas clouds in the volcano had no scent, neither did this soil. It did not make sense, and she was starting to feel irritated by things not making sense. *All the more reason to collect a sample for Eddie,* she told herself.

She pressed her shoulder against the trunk of one of the trees. The pressure she applied left an indent exactly like the one she had left in the stalk of the mushroom, the trunk of the magic tree, and the wall of the dome.

'Is everything in this place made of this rubbery stuff?' she called out.

'What?' Michael replied.

Molly decided not to shout back, but to keep going. She was close to one of the yellow balls and did not want to get distracted. She could see a tiny black dot on the top of the ball and thought Michael must have been right about it being a fertilizer release. But then the hole opened, and a burst of red light shot out of it.

Before Molly knew it, red lines were moving all around the botanical collective and a screeching sound sliced through the air. She shut her eyes tight and pressed her palms over her ears. The sound was awful. Then it changed to a series of *woop! woop! woop!* noises that were equally unpleasant. She felt as though the sound was slicing through every cell in her body, electrocuting her from the inside. And she clenched her jaw so hard that one of her baby teeth broke free from her gum and floated around the tip of her tongue. She spat the tooth onto the soil amidst a tiny blob of blood, then slowly crawled backward.

She felt a warm hand close around her ankle and pull her backward. Then she felt two hands grab her waist and pull her to a standing position. Relieved to see Michael's face, she let him take her hand. Together they ran down the path, straight toward the wall. They ran so fast, the surrounding plants soon appeared as a long blur of color.

Straight ahead, Molly could see the opaque white wall of the dome through the turquoise vine. The closer they got, the more she wondered about the wisdom of trying to jump through the wall. She knew the wall preferred a slow and gentle touch, so if she and Michael tried to run through it, they would surely be thrown back onto concrete path. And that would hurt.

Suddenly, the alarm stopped.

'Get ready!' Michael shouted, gripping Molly's hand even more tightly.

Then he charged, like a wild bull, straight into the wall.

Molly gasped as her chest slammed into the wall. It hurt, like falling belly first, into the swimming pool from the top diving board. She heard the familiar *pop!* as she entered. Then there was nothing. She did not move forward or backward. She was just there, inside the wall. And so was Michael.

'What's happening?' she whispered.

But the words did not escape her mouth. Her entire face, head, neck, and body were immobile. Only her eyes could move, and they moved just enough to see that Michael was not moving, either. Like her, his arms and legs were bent mid run, and they were going nowhere. Molly tried to move, but she was held in place by the thick, clear gel that filled the wall. She guessed the wall must was about half a meter thick, the same as the shield around the magic tree in her garden.

This must be what a fly feels like inside a spider's web, Molly thought. She moved her tongue around inside her mouth, then used it to push her lips open. Next, she opened her jaw. To her relief, the gel moved away, leaving a pocket of air for her to breathe.

'Where are we?' she asked.

Michael mumbled something, but his lips were still closed.

'Start with your lips and *then* your mouth,' Molly said.

Michael's lips moved, and then he gasped.

'We're stuck inside the wall,' he said.

'I'm aware of that,' Molly replied. 'But—'

She heard voices. Adult voices. They were shouting.

'The security company,' said Michael.

'What do you suppose they're shouting about?' Molly asked.

'They're probably trying to figure out who tripped the alarm,' Michael replied. 'I wish I could turn around and see them.'

'You will,' said Molly. 'Just take it slowly.'

She had full control over her head, face, and arms, so she looked over her shoulder.

'I can't see anyone,' she said.

She wriggled her toes.

'Oh no, I left my sandals between those rubbery trees!' she said.

'I left mine there, too,' said Michael.

Molly watched his moving, slowly.

'You look like someone doing Tai Chi,' she laughed.

'Over there!' someone shouted. 'The wall!'

Molly turned again, just in time to see a man running down the path.

'He has a gun!' she hissed.

'No way!' Michael shrieked.

'Shh,' Molly said.

'What difference does it make?' Michael snapped.

Molly watched, terrified, as the man got closer.

'I don't think he can see us,' she whispered.

A woman stepped out from behind the man. She, too,

was holding a gun, and she was staring at the wall, close to Molly and Michael.

'Somethin's goin' on there, for sure,' she said.

The security guards were so close, Molly could see the freckles on their sweaty faces.

'Look at their eyes,' Michael whispered. 'They can't see us.'

The man stepped back, staring at the wall and frowning. Then he lifted his gun, ready to fire.

'Oh, please God, no,' Molly whispered.

The female guard placed her hand on the man's arm until he lowered his gun.

'It's probably a thick blob of gel,' she said. 'After all, it is organic. Let's get back outside.'

Both guards put their guns in their holsters and stepped back, still staring at the wall. Behind them, Molly saw someone else approaching. It was a man and a dog.

'We're stuffed,' said Michael. 'There's no hiding from a German Shepherd.'

Molly hoped the gel would disguise their scent as well as it dulled their sound.

'I'm running out of air!' Michael gasped.

'No, you're having a panic attack,' said Molly. 'Slow down. Take deep breaths. Try to relax.'

Michael tried, but he sounded like a walrus on a windy day.

'Shh,' she whispered. 'Just focus on your breathing.'

She watched the dog approach, its nose leading the way and its sturdy body dragging the man along the concrete ground behind it. As it got closer, Molly could see the different coloured strands of the dog's fur. Black, white and brown. The beast was panting, and its tongue was hanging out of its mouth. Then it looked at the will, cocked its head to the side, and barked.

'What is it, mate?' the guard asked, placing a small treat on the dog's tongue.

The dog whined, then sat down, still staring at the wall. The guard stared at the wall, too.

'What is it?' he said again.

The dog stood up again and took a few steps closer to the wall, its nails clattering on the concrete path and its nose wriggling from side to side. Molly hoped the gel wall would resist the dog's teeth.

'What is it?' the guard asked again.

The dog whined again.

Michael sighed, then moved around. The dog snarled, its eyes fixed on a spot that was close to Michael's face. Then it barked with such force, the sound warbled through the gel. Molly felt it rippling around her body.

A second German Shepherd ran down the path toward them. Like the first, this one was dragging its human behind it. A moment later, there were two dogs staring at the wall, snarling, and barking. Molly could not take it anymore. She turned her back on them and stared through the other side of the wall.

But the view outside was worse. There she saw several dogs and guards wandering around the sinkhole, some wading knee-deep in the pool at the base of the waterfall.

'I can't take this anymore,' Michael cried.

'Me neither,' said Molly. 'We have to do something. We have to call Adali.'

'What?' said Michael, his face twisted into a knot.

'There's nothing else we can do!' Molly shouted, trying to be heard over the barking. 'Just put your hand on the wooden bird in your pocket and call for Adali!'

Michael scowled.

'Do it!' Molly shouted. 'Or I will never speak to you again!'

Michael wrapped his fingers around the wooden bird.

'Adali!' he cried. 'Please help us!'

31

ADALI'S MAGIC

Molly saw a bright white glow around the guards, their dogs and all the plants inside the dome.

'Can you see that?' she whispered, hearing her voice in slow motion.

'Yesss,' Michael replied, just as slowly.

Molly knew she was seeing the same bright white light she had seen in her garden the night Adali had revealed her magic and flown through the shield around the magic tree.

'Adali!' she sang out.

But her words were muffled by the gel which was also glowing. And it was softening and thinning, like cooking oil on a warm frypan. Molly looked at Michael. His face was relaxed and happy as Adali appeared in front of him. Her little brown wings beat so slowly, Molly could see the gel moving around them. It seemed to be obeying this tiny queen of the jungle.

Beyond the wall, Molly could see the waterfall outside,

no longer falling, but suspended in the air. It looked like a long, thick, white stripe down the granite wall. The pool was not moving, either. Its surface was broken, and the splashes made by the guards hung in midair.

She was about to look away when she saw a familiar shape. It was Jimbo. Leaning against the dark wall behind the waterfall, he was watching everything. When he had arrived, and what he was there for, Molly could not know. She only knew he was up to no good.

She returned her gaze to Adali. The bird's round black eyes moved from Michael's face to her own, then back again. Her beak was not moving, but Molly knew the bird was speaking to them.

'Wriggle down,' she said. 'There's only one way out, and it's down.'

Molly straightened her legs and pointed her toes toward the ground. Slowly the gel moved away from her, giving her room to push her pelvis forward and her feet backward.

'Relax. Let your body slide down to the ground,' said Adali.

Molly saw Michael wriggling down the inside of the wall, too.

'More,' said Adali.

Molly moved her pelvis forward and her feet backward as she had done before, then she reversed the action. Slowly, she was moving down. *I feel like a mermaid* she said without moving her mouth. Yet she knew that Adali and Michael had heard her.

'Soon you will move fast,' said Adali.

And she was right.

As soon as Molly's feet were level with the ground, everything changed. The gel pulled her under the ground so fast, she saw nothing but a solid stream of bright white light. She knew this was the mycelium network, but with one difference - she was inside it, not standing upon it as she had been during her last underground adventure.

She tried to be calm, but the experience was so strange, it was difficult. Her mind was racing with questions. *Where am I now? How much faster can I travel without dying? How long will this journey take? Where will it end?*

Molly felt herself being pulled upward. Feet first. A moment later, she heard the familiar *pop!* as she was flung out into the sunlight. She gulped in the fresh air and squinted under the light of the sun. A second later, Michael landed on the grass beside her.

'What the heck!' he shouted.

'There you are!' said Molly's father. 'I've been calling you for the last few minutes!'

Molly remembered her father's voice had been the last thing she had heard before she had stuck her finger into the hole in the side of the magic tree. She had done it to escape him. That had been several hours ago, so why he was saying 'the last few minutes' she could not fathom. She felt confused, but happy to see him.

She stared at the pink flowers on the hibiscus tree. Then she saw Adali, perched on a branch, staring at her. She waved at the bird, but the bird looked away.

'Molly!' her father called again, stepping toward her.

But Molly still could not answer. She stared at

Michael, hoping for some assurance that she was seeing and hearing everything properly, that this was not a dream. But Michael looked just as confused as she felt. Then, without a word, he ran back home.

'Molly,' her father said, helping her to her feet. 'What's going on with you?'

'Sorry, Dad,' Molly replied.

'You seem shocked,' said her father.

'Yeah,' was all she could say.

'Did something happen with Michael?' he asked, glancing toward the boy's house.

'No,' Molly replied. 'We were just doing some botanical science stuff.'

'What kind of stuff?' her father asked.

'Nothing much,' Molly said. 'Just counting the trees.'

She stood up and wrapped her arms around her father's waist, squeezing him so tight he would never be able to escape her.

'That's enough!' he said, wriggling free. 'You almost squashed my guts out!'

Molly laughed out loud.

'You're in a strange mood, muppet,' he said, ruffling her hair.

'Don't worry, Dad,' she replied. 'I'm just very happy to see you.'

'Good, because it's lunchtime,' he said. 'Please come inside.'

When they reached the top of the steps, Molly's father held the door open for her.

'After you, muppet,' he said.

Before Molly stepped inside, she took one last look at Adali the bird, sitting in the hibiscus tree.

I hope you enjoyed this book. If you would like to know what happens next, read the third and final book in this series. It's called Adaline's Magic.

www.ingramcontent.com/pod-product-compliance
Lightning Source LLC
Chambersburg PA
CBHW021438080526

44588CB00009B/576